Currency reform in
the Straits Settlements

J O Anthonisz

Currency Reform

in the

Straits Settlements

BY

J. O. ANTHONISZ, C.M.G.

Late Treasurer, Straits Settlements.

Richmond, London:

R. W. SIMPSON & CO., LTD., PRINTERS.

And may be obtained of

MESSRS JOHN LITTLE & CO., LTD, of Singapore and Kuala Lumpor,

and 10 Pancras Lane, Queen Street, London, E.C.

"The substitution of paper for the precious metals should always be carried as far as is consistent with safety; no greater amount of metallic currency being retained than is necessary to maintain, both in fact and in public belief, the convertibility of the paper."

JOHN STUART MILL,

"*Principles of Political Economy*"—*Book III, Chapter XXII.*

PREFACE.

THIS work was undertaken by me in consequence of the enquiries addressed to the Government of the Straits Settlements by foreign Governments and others for detailed information as to the measures taken for establishing a gold exchange standard in the Malay Peninsula. Although the operations in the Colony are on a small scale and sink into insignificance when compared with the magnitude of the operations conducted in India, the problems which have arisen are essentially the same, and the different method in which they have been handled by the Colonial authorities in some instances may prove of interest to currency experts. For the opinions expressed, where they diverge from the established practice, the responsibility is entirely mine. It is hoped that this record will be of some service particularly to my successors in office, and generally to those officials and unofficials in the Straits Settlements and Federated Malay States who may be called upon in the course of their duties to deal with currency questions.

J. O. ANTHONISZ.

CONTENTS

CHAPTER I

UP to the year 1903, the Colony of the Straits Settlements had no standard coin of its own. The Spanish dollar, which was introduced by the Portuguese, became the standard coin with the traders and the inhabitants of the then trading centre of the Malay Peninsula—Malacca,—and maintained its position as the favourite coin long after the introduction of the Mexican and South American dollars, which the restriction of the supply of the Spanish dollar and the expansion of trade had made necessary.

Notwithstanding the policy of the East India Company to dislodge the dollar and replace it with the rupee, it is worthy of note that the Spanish dollar retained its hold on the public as the standard coin, and the various substitutes for it, such as the Mexican dollar, the dollars of Peru and Bolivia, the Hong-Kong dollar, the American Trade dollar, the Japanese yen, and, finally, the British dollar, owing to their similarity to it in size, weight, and fineness, became current without very much difficulty, and maintained their position in the country as the equivalent of the standard coin.

For a proper understanding of the much-criticised proposal of the Straits Settlements Currency Committee of 1903, that a special Straits dollar of the same weight and fineness as the British dollar should be substituted for the Mexican and British dollars current in the Straits Settlements, it is necessary to describe the attitude of the community in the past in regard to the changes which took place by the natural process of events, or were made deliberately by governments in the standard coin of the country.

We find that, in the early days of the European colonization of Malacca, the community showed a decided preference for the dollar of Charles IV., and would not accept readily the dollar of Ferdinand VII. when it was first brought into circulation. It is also recorded that the dollars of Mexico and South America were, prior to 1808, regarded with suspicion, and passed at a discount of three to seven per cent., whereas the Carolus dollar of the same weight and fineness went at a premium of four to fifteen per cent. The Carolus " pillar " dollar, or, as the natives called it, the " cannon " dollar, long remained the favourite coin, until the difficulty of procuring it caused its disappearance from the market.

With the advent of the East India Company, the rupee was made legal tender, and the East India Company struck a special coinage to go with the rupee in their settlements, half and quarter rupees and copper money, one cent, half cent, and quarter cent pieces, the tin pice remaining in subsidiary circulation; but in Penang, although the rupee was the legal standard, all transactions were conducted in dollars, kupangs, and pice, which were also known as duits after the Netherlands-Indian coin, the " wang " and " wang bharu," other Netherlands-Indian coins, equivalent to four and five duits, also continued in circulation for a considerable period.*

Several attempts were made by the East India Company to oust the copper coins current in the Straits Settlements. The legislation introduced by them in 1835, as regards their rupee subsidiary coinage, failed to have any effect in the Settlements; and, in 1847, dollar cents, half cents, and quarter cents were issued. Again, in 1854, the East India Company endeavoured to force the rupee into circulation, by withholding the supply of dollar cents, half cents, and quarter cents, and substituting Indian copper coins, making them at the same time fractions of a dollar so as to facilitate the transaction. These measures were met with strenuous opposition, and had to be withdrawn. But a good deal of confusion remained—Government accounts were continued to be kept in rupees, annas, and pice, whereas all other accounts were were kept in dollars and cents. The whole of the revenue, except stamps, was collected in dollars and brought to account in rupees, annas, and pice, in Penang at a rate of Rs. 220 to $100, and in Singapore and Malacca at a rate based on this about

* $1 = 10 kupangs = 100 duits or pice.

Rs. 4½ higher, to cover, presumably, the cost of transport of the dollars. Salaries of officers were fixed in rupees, at a par of Rs. 220 to $100. For stamps a different rate obtained, as much as Rs. 7½ higher. This system was finally abolished in 1864, at the instance of Sir Hercules Robinson.

At the time of the transfer of the Straits Settlements to the Colonial Office, the Spanish, Mexican, Peruvian, Bolivian, and Hong-Kong dollar possessed the privilege of unlimited legal tender; but the Act (29 and 30 Vict. cap. 115), which made provision for the transfer of the Straits Settlements to the Colonial Office, enacted that the Governor in Council may from time to time notify any other silver dollar to be legal tender, which was of the same fineness as the Hong-Kong, and not less than 411 grains in weight; and an ordinance was passed in the Colony the same year, declaring that from the 1st of April, 1867, the Hong-Kong dollar, the silver dollar of Spain, Mexico, Peru, and Bolivia, and any other silver dollar to be specified from time to time by the Governor shall be the only legal tender. This ordinance repealed all the Indian Acts for making Indian coins legal tender.

The Hong-Kong Mint, which supplied the dollar of that name, and also the subsidiary silver and copper coins of the Straits Settlements, closed in 1868, after an existence of two years. The failure is ascribed to the high mint charges and low exchange. The Hong-Kong dollars were not accepted on the mainland of China under a discount of one per cent.

After the closing of the Mint, these dollars gradually went out of circulation.

In 1874, the American Trade dollar and the Japanese yen were made unlimited legal tender by an order of the Governor in Council, but were subsequently demonetised, the former in 1895, as it had ceased to be struck by the United States Government, and the latter in 1898 owing to the establishment of the gold standard in Japan and the demonetisation of the silver yen.

In 1890 all the orders regulating legal tender were repealed by an Order in Council, and the Mexican dollar was made the standard, the American Trade dollar, the Hong-Kong dollar and half dollar being made unlimited legal tender, and the subsidiary silver coins were made legal tender for two dollars and the copper coins legal tender for one dollar.

In 1895 the British trade dollar was introduced, owing to the scarcity of the Mexican dollars, on the recommendation of a Departmental Currency Committee appointed in 1893 by the Secretary of State for the Colonies, and was made legal tender in Hong-Kong, the Straits Settlements, and Labuan. By the orders of the Governor in Council of 1895 and 1898, the Mexican dollar was still maintained as the standard coin, and the British and Hong-Kong dollars were declared to be the equivalent of the standard. The first order demonetised the American Trade dollar and the second the Japanese yen.

As regards subsidiary coinage, there is no complete record of the silver coins struck prior to 1871. After the closing of the Hong-Kong Mint, arrangements were made with the Royal Mint to carry on the work, and since 1871 until very recently all subsidiary silver coins were struck at the Birmingham Mint. The twenty cent piece was the highest denomination until 1886, when a token fifty cent piece was introduced.

At the time, then, when measures were taken to make a Government issue of paper currency, the metallic currency consisted of unlimited legal tender dollars, mainly Mexican and British; subsidiary silver of the following denominations: fifty, twenty, ten, and five cent pieces; and copper coins, one cent, a large proportion of which were British North Borneo and Sarawak cents, and half cent and quarter cent pieces which were gradually disappearing, owing to the general rise of prices following the depreciation of the dollar. The dollars were imported by the Banks in response to public demand and the requirements of trade, the British dollars from the Bombay Mint and the Mexican dollars viâ San Francisco and London. The Government were only responsible for the subsidiary coin, and the profits from this coinage, which were considerable, were paid into revenue. This seemed such a sure and easy way of getting revenue that the administrations of the Malayan Native States, Perak, Selangor, and Negri Sambilan, which absorbed a considerable portion of this subsidiary coinage, claimed a portion of the profits, and were allowed the privilege of coining what was necessary for their requirements and of keeping the profits. This privilege was withdrawn after the establishment of the gold standard. In addition, there were bank notes issued by the Chartered Bank of India, Australia, and China, and the Hong Kong and Shanghai Bank. They were not legal tender, but were readily accepted.

The most important measure in the history of the Straits currency, before it was put on a gold basis, was undoubtedly the establishment of a Government Note Issue. The Colony is indebted to Sir Alexander Swettenham, the Colonial Secretary, and Mr. F. G. Penney, the Treasurer, for its successful inauguration. The Ordinance regulating the issue of Paper Currency was Ordinance No. 4 of 1899, and it followed the lines of the Ordinance provided for Ceylon by the Colonial Office. It was based on the principle that the reserve should fully cover the value of the notes issued. The reserve was kept partly in coin and partly in securities, the proportion fixed by law being a two-third minimum coin reserve and a one-third maximum security reserve. Discretionary power was given by the Ordinance to the Secretary of State to alter this proportion by public notification, and the reduction of the coin reserve to a minimum of one-half of the notes in circulation was sanctioned a few years after the passing of the Ordinance.

The income from investments was first applied to

defray the annually recurrent expenses of management, and to the payment of one per cent of the
cost price of the securities to a depreciation fund,
the balance being paid into revenue. The revenue,
however, had to make good every year, forthwith on
the order of the Governor, the amount of the
depreciation of the securities not covered by the
depreciation fund.

The notes authorised by the Ordinance were one
dollar notes with a limited legal tender of ten
dollars, and the following of unlimited legal tender :
five, ten, twenty, fifty, and one hundred dollar
notes, and any multiple of one hundred dollar notes.
The legal tender of these notes did not cover a
tender by the Currency Commissioners at their
office or a tender by the note-issuing Banks in
redemption of their own notes. Issues of five, ten,
twenty, fifty, and one hundred dollars were made at
the beginning, but no one dollar notes were issued
until 1905.

This summary, it is hoped, will sufficiently
explain the position of the currency of the Colony
when the arrangements for carrying into effect the
most important change of all—for placing the
currency on a gold basis—were begun.

It will be fitting to deal here with the causes
which originated the movement on the part of the
public in favour of putting the Straits currency on a
gold basis, and which impelled its growth in face of
much opposition from influential quarters, especially
of the Banking interest.

The adoption of the gold standard by Germany in 1872 led to large withdrawals of their silver coins from circulation ; and the French Mint, which had for nearly eighty years accepted silver at the rate of fifteen and a-half pounds of silver to one of gold. had to be closed to the silver of private holders. From that day the value of silver gradually declined, and with it the value of the dollar, until, from an exchange value in the neighbourhood of five shillings in 1872, it reached the value of 2/7⅜ in 1893. With the exception of complaints from individuals who had to make sterling remittances home, the grievances of public officials and others drawing fixed salaries, there was no general uneasiness. Merchants were able to find cover by making forward contracts, and to protect themselves from loss. Some took comfort in the hope that silver could not go on falling indefinitely, and that a reaction was bound to take place, and others in the popular belief that a depreciating currency simulated local produce, and that the profits from exports would leave more money for the purchase of imports and more than counterbalance the evil effects of the fall in the exchange value of the dollar.

In 1893, however, it was brought home to the Straits community that silver would go considerably lower, and was likely to stay there, by two momentous events in monetary history. In that year, in India, the Government closed their mints to the free coinage of rupees, and, in the United States, the Sherman Purchase Act, under which large accumulations of silver bullion had been made by periodical purchases, was repealed. It was considered time to take some action, and a committee was appointed by Sir Cecil Clementi-Smith, the then Governor, composed of Government officials, merchants, and representatives of the Chinese community, to receive the views of representative men of all classes and to suggest remedial measures. Half of the members of this committee were in favour of extending the Indian currency to the Straits Settlements, but the other half, including all the Chinese members, were in favour of the maintenance of a silver standard. They however, recommended that a British dollar of the same weight and fineness as the Mexican dollar should be supplied by Government. The opinion expressed by the only Banker on this committee, in a separate minute, is fairly typical of the attitude taken up by the Banks throughout this controversy. He concludes as follows: " I am in favour of a British dollar following silver as being likely to give impetus to planting enterprise and production generally in the Malay Peninsula, but the Government, before introducing such a coin, must clearly decide never to make it a token." The suggestion, apparently was that the Government should control the supply of the dollar by confining the coinage to silver purchased by them. The British dollar introduced on the recommendation of the Departmental Committee appointed by the Secretary of State was, however, obtainable by everyone who chose to send silver to the Bombay Mint.

No further representations from the public appear to have been made to the Government until 1897. The rate of exchange in 1892 (2/7⅜) had by then gone down to 1/11$\frac{15}{16}$. In the meantime it is significant that large bodies of wage-earners had succeeded in impressing the justice of their claims on their employers. Government servants with a European domicile were granted exchange compensation, viz., half their salaries were paid to them at the rate of three shillings to the dollar, and a few years after the whole of their salaries were paid at that rate ; the municipalities followed suit, and all the Banks, some of the mercantile firms, and the Dock Company gave increases to their employees much on the same lines. Officers and engineers on local steamers secured by a strike a considerable rise in their salaries. Professional men raised their charges, and approval was given by the authorities to an increase in solicitors' fees. As regards the income of natives, I take the following statement from a report of a Sub-Committee of the Singapore Chamber of Commerce, appointed in 1897, specially to inquire into the local currency with a view to calling the attention of the Government to the question of converting the Straits currency to a gold standard : " It would appear that the wages of Chinese immigrants have not risen, in any appreciable degree, during the past seven years. This coincides with what has come to be regarded as one of the most important features in our import trade with gold standard countries, viz., that the income of natives generally is not elastic, and has not kept pace with the rise in prices caused by the depreciation of the dollar."

However correct this statement may be in respect of contract coolies—and the statement is based on information colleoted from the contract registers at the Chinese Protectorate—it cannot be said to apply to the majority of the old resident labourers in the Colony. The fact remains that wages of domestic servants went up enormously long before their employers received any compensation, and it formed one of the reasons for granting compensation. The assertion, so frequently made by men of influence and experience that the depreciation of the exchange value of the dollar had not affected its purchasing power in relation to local articles, had come to be accepted as an uncontrovertible fact, and was the reason why a much smaller compensation in proportion to their salaries was given, and at a much later date, to the local men employed by the Government, Municipalities, firms, and other employers. An instructive and an interesting proof to the contrary is furnished by the gradual disappearance from the markets of the Colony of the quarter and half cent pieces, which financed all the pettier purchases of the neccessaries of Eastern life. But, although compensation was given by all employers who were able to afford it, the question was as far removed from a satisfactory solution as ever. The Sub-Committee of the Chamber of Commerce, already referred to, found that, for the great majority of employers, no compensation in any shape or form seemed warranted by the present position of business affairs in the Colony, and fixity of exchange on some distinctly higher basis than the present had become with them an urgent necessity. The Sub-Committee recommended the adoption of the English sovereign as the basis of the currency with a Straits dollar, fixed at two shillings, subsidiary to it, the present subsidiary silver coinage to remain as it was. The *modus operandi* suggested was that a law should be passed at one sitting of the Legislative Council, and simultaneously in the Federated Malay States, without letting the intentions of Government becoming known, that a notice be issued that, within a period of time sufficiently brief to prevent importation, all dollars then circulating in the Colony and the Federated Malay States would be exchanged for currency notes, and that Goverment should raise a loan In London and import a gold reserve in sovereigns. The question, having been submitted in this concrete form to the Straits Government, was then referred to the authorities of the Federated Malay States for their views and the views of the representatives of the different communities there. Two of the Residents declared in favour of a gold standard. European planters and miners appeared to be equally divided on the subject, but the United Planters' Association passed a resolution objecting to fixity of exchange on the ground that it was undesirable in the interests of the planting community. The Chinese generally were reported as being probably in favour of the silver standard. The Resident-General, Sir Frank Swettenham, afterwards Governor of the Straits Settlements, was in favour of a gold standard with a silver token dollar, as recommended by the Singapore Chamber of Commerce. The question remained in abeyance until 1902, when Sir Frank Swettenham, who had succeeded to the Governorship, requested the Secretary of State to refer the question to an expert, preferably with Indian experience; and, as a result of this application, a committee was appointed in London with Sir David Barbour as President. This committee will be referred to in this work as the Straits Settlements Currency Committee.

When the fact became known that this committee had been appointed, numerous petitions were sent in from all classes of the community declaring in favour of putting the currency on a gold basis. The most important of these was a general petition signed by all the firms and public companies in the Colony, by employees, both European and native, and also, by a very large number of wealthy and influential Chinese, revenue farmers, shipowners, bankers, merchants, and landowners. All the representatives in London and on the Continent of Straits Settlements firms also forwarded petitions to the Committee in favour of a gold standard. The Singapore and Penang Chambers of Commerce, the Municipality of Singapore, and the Federated Malay States Planters' Association* made representations to the same effect. A petition signed by nearly all the principal Asiatic traders of Penang also asked for a gold standard. On tne other hand, a large majority of the miners expressed a preference for a silver standard, and a numerously-signed petition, almost exclusively Chinese, was presented to the Legislative Council by the only European unofficial member who was opposed to the adoption of a gold standard. It was clear, beyond doubt, that the weight of opinion was strongly in favour of a gold standard as the only possible method of bringing about stability of exchange.

The Straits Settlements Currency Committee issued their report in May, 1903. As to the expediency of the change, after setting out the arguments for and against it, they made this very guarded statement: " While we do not think that a gold standard should be pressed on the Straits Settlements against the wishes of the Government and the people, we are equally of opinion that no objection should be raised on the part of His Majesty's Government to the principle of the change, if the Government of the Straits Settlements, after considering all sides of the question,

* The change of opinion on the part of the Association was probably due to the difficulty of getting capital out from England.

should decide finally in favour of an alteration from the silver to the gold standard."

It can be seen from the report that the importance of the principle that the Government should only give the people the form of currency for which they ask was the dominating feature of their scheme, and has a material bearing on the recommendations made by them. It was partly on this account, and partly on account of the inconvenience that would be caused in changing the system of accounts to a rupee basis, that the Straits Settlements Currency Committee rejected the proposal for the extension of the currency of India to the Colony, a proposal which was advocated by a section of the Currency Committee appointed by the Governor in 1893. The same reason made them put aside the scheme of the Sub-Committee of the Singapore Chamber of Commerce appointed in 1897. They considered that the risk of its failure, owing to the possible suspicion and opposition on the part of the native population to a wholesale substitution of notes for dollars, was so great that they could not recommend its adoption.

The plan which they recommended was :—

(1) Gradually to introduce a dollar of the same weight and fineness as the British dollar current in the East to be substituted for the Mexican and British dollars circulating in the Colony, the latter dollars being demonetised as soon as the supply of the new dollars was sufficient to permit of this being done with safety. They suggested that a portion of

the coin reserve held against the note issue should be melted down and converted into the new Straits dollars.

(2) That, with the arrival of the first supply of the new dollars, they should be made legal tender and their export prohibited, and that the import of British and Mexican dollars should temporarily be prohibited.

(3) When the currency was largely composed of the new dollars, the British and Mexican dollars should finally be demonetised.

(4) After sufficient dollars had been coined to meet the requirements of business in the currency area, the coinage of dollars would cease, until the exchange value of the dollar had reached whatever value in relation to the sovereign might be decided on by the Government as the future value of the Straits' dollar. After this stage was reached, the Government would issue the new dollars in exchange for gold at the fixed rate.

(5) When the gold standard was established, it would not be indispensable that any gold coins should be made legal tender in the Colony and in the Federated Malay States; but the Government should be prepared not only to give dollars in exchange for sovereigns at the declared rate, but also to give sovereigns in exchange for dollars at the same rate, so long as gold was available, or to give bills on the Crown agents in London based on this rate.

Measures were immediately taken to carry these recommendations into effect. Arrangements were

made with the Indian Government for the Bombay
Mint to undertake the coinage of the new Straits
dollar. The design of the new dollar was decided
upon, and an Order was made by the King in
Council on 25th June, 1903, empowering the
Governor, with the consent of the Secretary of State,
to make this dollar legal tender, by proclamation, in
the Colony, and to declare that Mexican and British
dollars shall cease to be legal tender. In July, the
Currency Note Ordinance was amended to allow of
coin being taken out of the Note Guarantee Fund
for the purpose of reminting. By the middle of
August, dollars to the amount of two and a-half
millions had been shipped to Bombay, and the
Banks were also given permission to ship a limited
number of British and Mexican dollars under
Government supervision to the Bombay Mint,
which was specially authorised to receive them.
As soon as these operations were undertaken, it
became known at large that the Government of the
Straits Settlements purposed recoining all the
British and Mexican dollars current in the Colony
and the Federated Malay States. Sterling exchange
was at the time higher in the Straits than in China
and Indo-China, and the Mexican and British
dollars began to flow in in considerable quantities,
being imported by the Banks and by Chinese
speculators. The Government were strongly urged
to prohibit forthwith the further importation of these
dollars, but, as the new dollars were not ready, they
properly declined to take any action beyond warning

the public that they would give no pledge that new dollars would, ultimately, be given for all Mexican and British dollars current in the Straits Settlements and Federated Malay States, and beyond taking steps to introduce an Ordinance to regulate the import and export of coin into and from the Colony.* This Ordinance empowered the Governor, with the approval of the Secretary of State, to prohibit the importation of any coin, whether legal tender or not, and the exportation of any coin which was legal tender in the Colony; and, also, to exempt any particular country or state from the operation of any such order. The latter power made it possible to put the States of the Malay Peninsula on a different footing from that of other foreign countries in the matter of currency.

The first supply of the new dollars arrived at the end of September, 1903, and the following proclamations and orders of the Governor in Council were issued, under the authority of the King's Order in Council of 25th June, 1903 :—

(1) Proclamation dated 2nd October, 1903, declaring the Straits Settlements dollar legal tender from 3rd October, 1903.

(2) Order of the Governor in Council prohibiting the importation of the British and Mexican dollars from 3rd October, 1903.

(3) Order of the Governor in Council prohibiting the exportation of the Straits Settlements dollars from 3rd October, 1903.

* Ordinance xxiv. of 1903.

(4) Order of the Governor in Council exempting the Federated Malay States and Johore from the operation of the two last preceding orders.

(5) Proclamation dated the 5th October, 1903, constituting the new Straits dollar the standard coin of the Colony.

Notices in Malay, Chinese, and Tamil were posted up throughout the Colony, the Federated Malay States and Johore announcing these currency changes.

In addition to these measures, instructions were given not to make remittances from the coin reserve of the Currency Commissioners for investment in England or India, as this would mean throwing fresh money on the market, and would retard the contraction of the currency in circulation which was necessary for carrying out the proposals of the Straits Settlements Currency Committee.

With the cessation of the coinage of dollars except by Government, and the prohibition of the importation of the other legal tender dollars current in the Colony and the Federated Malay States, the first steps were taken to dissociate the Straits currency from a silver basis. The course of exchange (telegraphic transfer rates) as compared with Hong-Kong, and the average spot price of silver in London are shown in the following table on pages 22 and 23.

This table may be summarised as follows:—In the last three months in 1903, whilst silver fell from $27\frac{7}{8}$ to $25\frac{3}{4}$, the dollar in Hong-Kong fell from $22\frac{9}{16}$

to $20\frac{3}{8}$, and the dollar in the Straits from $23\frac{5}{16}$ to $20\frac{15}{16}$. In 1904, silver fell from $26\frac{7}{16}$ to $24\frac{31}{32}$ between January and April, the dollar in Hong-Kong fell from $23\frac{1}{4}$ to $20\frac{5}{8}$, and the dollar in the Straits ranged between $23\frac{9}{16}$ and $21\frac{9}{16}$. The lowest limit reached in the Straits was when silver was at $26\frac{7}{16}$ during this period. During the remainder of the year, silver rose from $25\frac{3}{8}$ in May to $27\frac{7}{8}$ in December, the dollar in Hong-Kong rose from $21\frac{5}{16}$ to $23\frac{9}{16}$, and the dollar in the Straits from $21\frac{1}{2}$ to $23\frac{1}{2}$. It will be seen from the following table that, in December, 1904, when silver was at $27\frac{7}{8}$, the Hong-Kong rate was one-sixteenth higher than the Singapore rate. From December, 1904, to February, 1905, the price of silver rose from $27\frac{7}{8}$ to $28\frac{1}{16}$, Hong-Kong exchange rose from $22\frac{13}{16}$ to $24\frac{1}{16}$ in January, and fell to $23\frac{11}{16}$. Singapore kept pace with silver, and rose uniformly from $23\frac{1}{4}$ to $23\frac{13}{16}$. The price of silver dropped again in March, 1905, reaching $26\frac{1}{16}$ in April, whence it rose again to $27\frac{3}{4}$ in August. Hong-Kong exchange dropped with it, and remained in the neighbourhood of $22\frac{3}{4}$ till July, rising to $23\frac{3}{8}$ in August, whereas Singapore kept at a level of $23\frac{7}{8}$, reaching $24\frac{1}{16}$ in July and $25\frac{7}{16}$ in August. Silver rose steadily from $28\frac{17}{32}$ in September to $29\frac{31}{32}$ in December. Hong-Kong exchange rose from $22\frac{15}{16}$ to $25\frac{1}{16}$ and Singapore from $25\frac{5}{16}$ to $26\frac{5}{8}$.

The course of exchange, as compared with the bullion value of silver, did not give any conclusive or even satisfactory indication that the exchange value of the dollar had been completely separated

Date	Singapore—sterling exchange.		Hongkong—sterling exchange		Average price of standard silver.
	Max.	Min	Max	Min	
1903 October ...	$23\frac{5}{16}$	$22\frac{13}{16}$	$22\frac{9}{16}$	$22\frac{1}{8}$	$27\frac{7}{8}$
November ...	$22\frac{7}{8}$	$21\frac{7}{16}$	$22\frac{1}{16}$	$20\frac{7}{8}$	$27\frac{1}{32}$
December ...	$21\frac{15}{16}$	$20\frac{15}{16}$	$20\frac{7}{8}$	$20\frac{3}{8}$	$25\frac{3}{4}$
1904 January ...	$22\frac{5}{16}$	$21\frac{8}{16}$	$22\frac{3}{4}$	$20\frac{7}{8}$	$26\frac{7}{16}$
February ...	$23\frac{9}{16}$	$21\frac{15}{16}$	$23\frac{1}{4}$	$21\frac{3}{4}$	$26\frac{9}{16}$
March ...	$23\frac{1}{4}$	$22\frac{7}{16}$	$22\frac{1}{2}$	$21\frac{7}{16}$	$26\frac{1}{4}$
April ...	$22\frac{15}{16}$	$21\frac{15}{16}$	$21\frac{3}{4}$	$20\frac{5}{8}$	$24\frac{31}{32}$
May ...	$22\frac{15}{16}$	$21\frac{1}{2}$	$21\frac{3}{4}$	$21\frac{5}{16}$	$25\frac{3}{8}$
June ...	$23\frac{7}{16}$	$22\frac{3}{4}$	$22\frac{1}{8}$	$21\frac{9}{16}$	$25\frac{19}{32}$
July ...	$23\frac{7}{16}$	$23\frac{1}{4}$	$22\frac{7}{16}$	22	$26\frac{29}{32}$
August ...	$23\frac{3}{8}$	23	$22\frac{5}{8}$	$21\frac{9}{16}$	$26\frac{23}{32}$
September ...	$23\frac{1}{16}$	$22\frac{11}{16}$	$22\frac{3}{16}$	$21\frac{5}{8}$	$26\frac{11}{32}$
October ...	$23\frac{3}{16}$	$22\frac{15}{16}$	$22\frac{3}{16}$	$21\frac{15}{16}$	$26\frac{3}{4}$
November ...	$23\frac{1}{4}$	$23\frac{3}{16}$	$22\frac{13}{16}$	$22\frac{1}{4}$	$26\frac{15}{16}$

Date	Singapore—sterling exchange.		Hongkong—sterling exchange.		Average price of standard silver.
	Max	Min	Max	Min	
1904 December ...	$23\frac{1}{2}$	$23\frac{1}{4}$	$23\frac{9}{16}$	$22\frac{13}{16}$	$27\frac{7}{8}$
1905 January ...	$23\frac{9}{16}$	$23\frac{7}{16}$	$24\frac{1}{16}$	$23\frac{7}{16}$	$27\frac{31}{32}$
February ...	$23\frac{13}{16}$	$23\frac{9}{16}$	$23\frac{11}{16}$	$22\frac{5}{8}$	$28\frac{1}{16}$
March ...	$23\frac{3}{4}$	$23\frac{9}{16}$	$22\frac{5}{8}$	$22\frac{1}{16}$	$26\frac{7}{8}$
April ...	$23\frac{9}{16}$	$23\frac{7}{16}$	$22\frac{7}{16}$	$21\frac{13}{16}$	$26\frac{1}{16}$
May ...	$23\frac{7}{8}$	$23\frac{1}{2}$	$22\frac{3}{4}$	$22\frac{5}{16}$	$26\frac{5}{8}$
June ...	$23\frac{13}{16}$	$23\frac{5}{8}$	$22\frac{5}{8}$	$22\frac{1}{4}$	$26\frac{15}{16}$
July ...	$24\frac{1}{16}$	$23\frac{13}{16}$	$22\frac{3}{4}$	$22\frac{7}{16}$	$27\frac{5}{32}$
August ...	$25\frac{7}{16}$	$24\frac{1}{16}$	$23\frac{3}{8}$	$22\frac{5}{8}$	$27\frac{3}{4}$
September ...	$25\frac{5}{8}$	$25\frac{5}{16}$	$23\frac{7}{16}$	$22\frac{15}{16}$	$28\frac{17}{32}$
October ...	$25\frac{5}{8}$	$25\frac{5}{16}$	$23\frac{11}{16}$	$23\frac{5}{16}$	$28\frac{5}{8}$
November ...	$26\frac{1}{16}$	$25\frac{5}{8}$	$25\frac{1}{8}$	$23\frac{5}{8}$	$29\frac{13}{32}$
December ...	$26\frac{5}{8}$	$25\frac{15}{16}$	$25\frac{1}{16}$	$24\frac{1}{4}$	$29\frac{31}{32}$
1906 January ...	$28\frac{3}{4}$	$26\frac{5}{8}$	$24\frac{13}{16}$	$24\frac{17}{32}$	$30\frac{1}{8}$

from silver.   It is true that during the period, March to June, 1905, whereas the price of silver was low, Straits exchange kept at a much higher level than Hong-Kong, and above the bullion value of the dollar.   This is the only indication afforded us that the Straits currency was following a course separate from silver.

*The situation was complicated by the large speculations of a foreign banker and certain merchants, some of whom speculated on a half-crown dollar being fixed, and some on a double rupee (2/8) value being given to the dollar, whilst others based their calculations on the advance in the price of silver making it impossible for the Government to provide a sufficient margin of safety between the melting point of the dollar and the nominal value of two shillings which it was generally believed and desired that the dollar would be fixed at.

There are also other other factors which should

---

*It was generally reported and believed that this Bank succeeded in making a corner in dollars and notes, and that the difference between the value of the dollars when this Bank received them and the fixed value of 2/4, which should have accrued to Government in the form of seignorage, went into the coffers of the Bank.   This is very far from the truth.   The profits were chiefly book profits, a large part of which the Bank was unable to collect.   In fact, the Bank ran short of local currency, and had to beg help from the other Banks to replenish its coffers.   On one occasion, when further assistance was refused, except at exorbitant rates, this Bank was compelled to purchase local currency from the Currency Commissioners at the gold import point $2/4\frac{5}{16}$ which was then $2/4\frac{5}{16}$ when the Banks' selling rate was quoted at 2/4.

be taken into consideration. If we study the course of exchange as given in the table, we see that the dollar rose on two occasions out of all proportion to the price of silver; and though it is true that a currency based on silver generally follows the fortunes of silver, abnormal rises take place in the exchange value of a currency if there is an insufficient supply of it to meet the requirements of trade, so that if the Banks delay to import, or find difficulty in getting sufficient currency coined, and thus delay the importation of currency to meet a favourable balance of trade, a sharp rise in exchange will take place. In the same way abnormal falls will occur if there is any undue delay or difficulty in the liquidation of debts due to an unfavourable trade balance.

In the midst of these fluctuations due to such various causes, and a rising market in silver which made it difficult for the Government to arrive at a sure judgment as to whether the value of the dollar had been totally separated from the value of silver,

---

Though no seignorage profits accrued to Government from this scheme, all the Government deposits in the Banks and Treasuries appreciated in gold value, whereas, on the other hand, their sterling and Indian investments depreciated to a like extent in dollar value. Had it not been for the payment of the Tanjong Pagar Dock Award, which was given in dollars, the balance would have been in favour of the Government. The losers were those who had invested their dollar savings outside the Colony in gold-using countries, and the gainers those who had invested capital in the Colony and the Federated Malay States. The chief losers were the Currency Commissioners, most of whose sterling investments showed a considerably smaller dollar equivalent.

the Straits Settlements Government were confronted with the problem of either fixing the dollar finally, or of giving temporary relief by exchanging dollars for gold at current Bank rates, and indefinitely postponing fixity of exchange. Special legislation had been introduced in March, 1904 (Ordinance IV. of 1904), to enable the Currency Commissioners to issue notes in Singapore against gold tendered to the Crown Agents for the Colonies in London at a rate of exchange to be notified by an order of the Governor in Council with the previous approval of the Secretary of State. This section was intended to give the Government the means of preventing any inconvenient rise in the current rate of exchange before the time arrived for fixing the value of the dollar. This power was never made use of. In the repeal of this section by Ordinance III. of 1905, passed in March, 1905, and the substitution for it of a section providing that gold shall be received in Singapore as well as in London in exchange for notes, and the manner in which it should be used, the original object of this section was apparently lost sight of, and when the time came when it became necessary to relieve the situation, the community were decidedly opposed to a further indefinite prolongation of the state of suspense and uncertainty which had proved so encouraging to speculation and so inimical to legitimate enterprise. Finality was demanded, and finality was given.

The policy adopted by India of declaring in advance the value at which the rupee was to be fixed, was not followed in the Straits Settlements. The Straits Settlements Currency Committee were intentionally silent on the question of the value to be given to the dollar, as they considered that it was a matter for the Government to decide in the light of further experience. It was thought that any premature announcement as to the future gold value of the dollar might promote speculation and have a mischievous effect, and that it would be best not to attempt to fix the value of the new dollar at first, but to leave that important point to be decided in the light of the experience that would be gained when further coinage was stopped. The Singapore Chamber of Commerce asked for a two-shilling dollar, and the majority of the witnesses, connected with the Straits, who gave evidence before the Straits Settlements Currency Committee also declared in favour of a two-shilling dollar, and there is no doubt that the authorities, both in the Colony and in England, inclined to this value being given to the dollar.

With a view to avoiding interference with the status of existing contracts, and to obviating hardship in the relations between debtor and creditor, the Straits Settlements Currency Committee made it one of the essential features of their scheme that the dollar should, when fixed, be approximately the current rate of exchange at the time of fixing. The history of the currency of the Straits Settlements has been, since 1872, one of continual fluctuations as regards its exchange value, and the community had become accustomed to adapting their transactions accordingly. There could be no reasonable grounds for complaint if an average rate based on the fluctuations of the preceding ten or fifteen years were selected and the dollar fixed at that figure when the rate of exchange either rose or fell to it. There would have been grave injustice if the unit of value had been arbitrarily fixed without regard to these considerations, and special legislation would have been found necessary to protect the interests of debtor and creditor. It was not considered that this question was likely to arise out of the scheme propounded by the Straits Settlements Currency Committee, and this opinion was justified after fixity became an established fact.

Such being the plan, the price of silver and the course of exchange were carefully watched, and, as early as July, 1904, representations were made to the authorities at home. The opinion of the experts consulted was, that, notwithstanding the continuance of the Russo-Japanese War, silver was likely to fall; and, though the outlook even then appeared to be very much against fixing the value of the dollar so low as two shillings, in view of the rising market in silver it was considered undesirable to take any steps to fix exchange, as, owing to the rise in the price of silver, the appreciation of the dollar would have taken place, even if no currency scheme had been initiated.

The final stage of the measures necessary to contract the currency was reached in August, 1904.

By the first week in August 29,975,000 of the new dollars had reached the Colony, large enough to meet all the currency requirements of the Colony and the Federated Malay States, and it was considered safe to demonetise the British, Mexican, and Hong Kong dollar. This was done by proclamation on the 24th of August, 1904.

An examination of the table given above will show that the demonetisation of the old dollar did not result in any appreciable rise in the rate of exchange. The rates from September, 1904 to June, 1905, were fairly steady, keeping between a minimum of $22\frac{11}{16}$ (September, 1904) and a maximum of $23\frac{7}{8}$ (May, 1905), the price of silver being respectively $26\frac{11}{32}$ and $26\frac{5}{8}$ per standard ounce.

In the middle of 1904, there was considerable depression of trade in the Colony, and, though some observers were inclined to attribute it to the currency changes introduced by Government, there was nothing in their features to distinguish the failures which then took place from the far more serious failures of the previous decade. It may be seen from the reports of the Official Assignee and the Chambers of Commerce that these periods of depression occur with periodical regularity, and invariably follow periods of prosperity. In prosperous times it is easy to get credit, speculation sets in, credit is extended where it is already inflated ; when the collapse comes there is an undue restriction, although many failures could be averted by a prudent extension of credit, such as was the case when the European Banks and firms stopped advances and sales on credit, and many Chinese, firms were only saved from bankruptcy by the action of the Chetties, the Indian moneylenders, who found it profitable to come to their rescue. There do not seem to me any grounds for the belief which many people entertained that the currency changes were responsible for the depression which took place in 1904. There was no such marked stringency of local currency as to prevent the Banks giving their usual credit, and in 1905, it was the opinion of some of the leading business firms that no contraction of currency had yet taken place at Singapore which could be felt by the business community.

However, in the middle of 1905, there was a marked revival of the produce business in the Colony and the Federated Malay States. The price of tin began to rise, and considerable outside capital came into the country for investment in rubber. With a closed currency, with no means of expansion open to the public either by the tender of gold or silver, this increase of the export trade formed a most powerful factor in enhancing the value of the dollar, much more so, in my opinion, than the rise in the price of silver.

In July, 1905, exchange (demand) rose to 2/0$\frac{1}{8}$, and it was generally expected that, owing to the revival of the produce business, it would rise over 2/1 before the end of the year. The proposal to fix the dollar at 2/- was reluctantly abandoned. In fixing the dollar under the scheme of the Straits Settlements

Currency Committee two essential conditions had
to be complied with. A sufficient margin had to be
left between the token value and the bullion value
of the dollar so as to save it from the melting pot,
and the value of the dollar had to be as near as
possible the current rate of exchange. The following
proposals were then submitted for consideration,
the main object being to keep the value of the
dollar as low as possible consistent with safety, and
to fix it whenever the market rate of exchange
approached approximately the rate decided upon.

The first proposal was based on one of the
recommendations of the American Commission that
the unit of value to be adopted in the Far Eastern
countries, which had decided on going in for a gold
standard, should be as uniform as possible, and that
the value should be fixed at or near the coinage
ratio of 32 (silver) to 1 (gold). This was approximately the ratio adopted in the Philippines for their
peso. This was also approximately the ratio on
which the Japanese silver half-yen was based. If
the silver unit were 480 grains, the gold unit would
be 15 grains. Working this out for the Straits
dollar (416 grains and 900 fineness) and the
sovereign as unit (123·27447 grains), the value of
the Straits dollar would have come to $2/1\frac{5}{16}$,
approximately. The advantages claimed for adopting this coinage ratio in conjunction with the
neighbouring countries which had also gone in for a
gold standard, were that there would be less danger
of other countries giving a higher value to silver by

continuing to purchase above our limit of value; that the purchase of silver bullion would be automatically suspended at practically the same points; when the countries interested stopped purchasing, the tendency to a rise in the price of silver would be effectually arrested, and that the demand for silver would be so distributed that it would be possible to regulate its price and maintain its stability. One very important factor was overlooked in these calculations, and that was the cheapening of the price of gold by over-production. The subsequent rise in the price of silver, which was to a large extent due to the depreciation of gold, compelled Japan and the Philippines to recoin their silver currency at a very much smaller coinage ratio.

The upward movement in the price of silver soon made it evident that the value recommended of $2/1\frac{1}{2}$ for the dollar was too low, and that the margin between this and bullion par was not sufficiently safe. An exchange of nine dollars to the sovereign was then suggested, and was accepted as a more convenient rate providing a sufficient margin of safety. By the middle of November, however, when this rate was agreed to, exchange (telegraphic transfer) had risen to 2/2, and the price of silver had also risen to well over 29d. per ounce. It was then proposed to reduce the dollar to 800 fineness, so as to ensure a fixed value of $9 to £1 without running the risk of the exportation of our dollars for sale as bullion. This proposal was not agreed to, as it

FLUCTUATIONS OF EXCHANGE IN JANUARY 1906

BEFORE THE DOLLAR WAS FIXED AT $2/4\frac{1}{4}$ ON THE $29\frac{th}{}$ JANUARY.

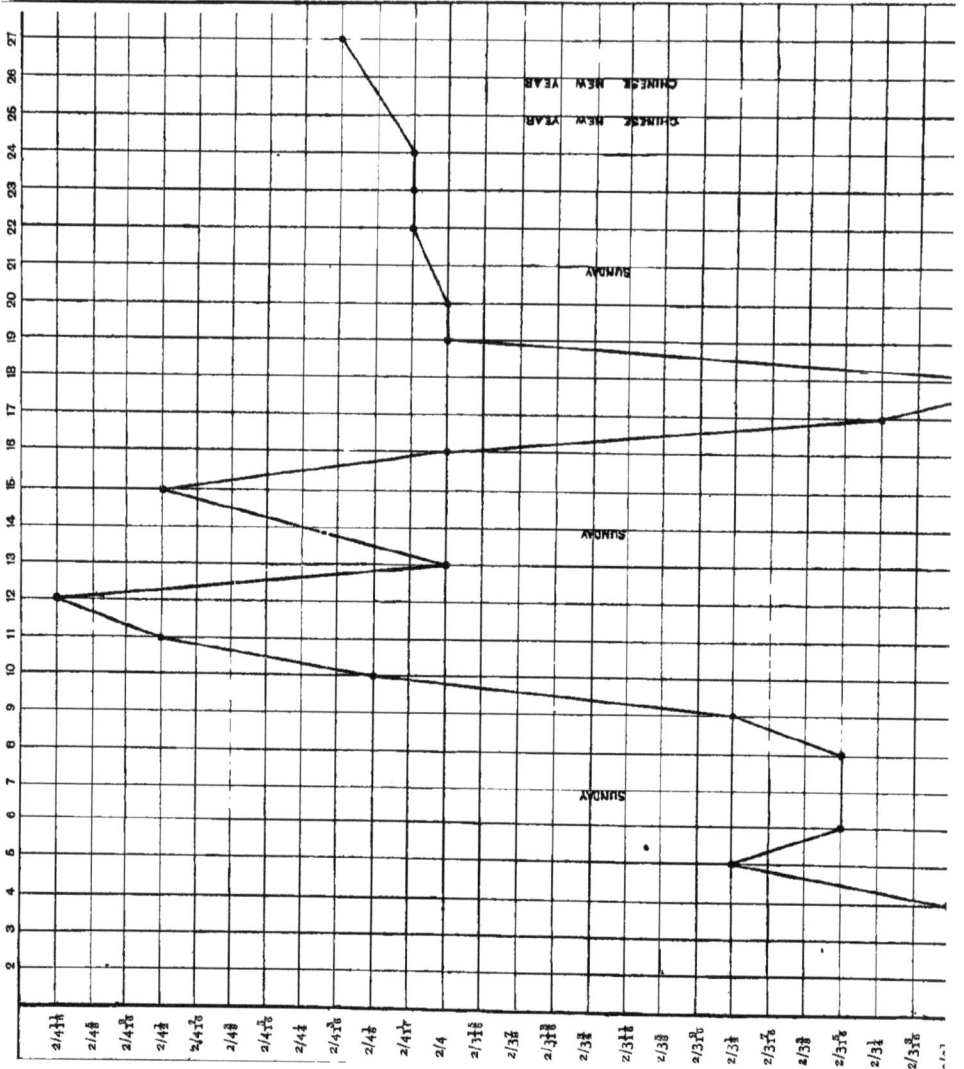

meant such a wide departure from the proposals of the Straits Settlements Currency Committee. It was considered that it would certainly be necessary to seek further expert advice, and to arrive at a general concurrence before adopting so wide a departure from the accepted scheme.

In December, 1905, the telegraphic rate of exchange rose to 2/2$\frac{5}{8}$, only $\frac{1}{24}$th of a penny below the proposed rate of $9 to £1. Here, then, was the opportunity to fix the dollar at this rate according to the scheme of the Straits Settlements Currency Committee; but, owing to the steady rise of the price of silver, no action was taken. The opinion held was that the time for action would come when a decided fall in the price of silver set in again.

In January, 1906, preparations had to be made for the supply of local currency to meet the customary requirements of the Chinese New Year, which fell on the 25th of the month. This, coming on the top of wide-spread speculation in exchange, which had been going on for some months past and were coming due for settlement, unsettled the market and put a stop to nearly all legitimate business. Exchange fluctuated by leaps and bounds, and widely different rates from the opening rates were quoted by the banks in the course of the same day. There were sometimes five or six quotations a day. The diagram annexed will give some idea of the fluctuations of exchange between the 2nd and 27th of January, confined though it is to the opening rates for each day. On the 12th of the month the Governor, Sir John Anderson, spoke at a meeting of the Legislative Council, and warned the public against the unauthorised rumours as to the intentions of the Government as regards the exchange value to be given to the dollar, stating that the Government's desire was to fix the dollar as low as possible consistently with safety. The result was that the dollar dropped from $2/4\frac{11}{16}$ to 2/4 on the following day. It rose again to $2/4\frac{1}{2}$ and dropped to 2/3 in the course of three days. The next day it rose again, and continued to rise until it reached $2/4\frac{3}{16}$ on the 27th of January. Owing to the uncertainty of the outlook, nearly all legitimate business was stopped, and it became impossible for the Government to consider tenders for important and urgent public works. It was felt that any risk of failure to maintain a fixed rate was far preferable to the loss to the community and the Government by a prolongation of this uncertainty. Representations were again made to the Secretary of State urging fixity.

Silver had now reached the price $30\frac{1}{4}$d. per ounce, and it was evident that the margin of safety for a dollar value based on the ratio of \$9 to £1, viz., $2/2\frac{2}{3}$, was much too narrow. Besides, the market rate of exchange had long since gone beyond this value. Permission was, accordingly, granted to the dollar being fixed at 2/4, which was considered the lowest rate possible, consistent with safety. At this time the Bank rate stood at $2/4\frac{1}{8}$, and showed a tendency to go higher. As it was not possible to make the necessary arrangements for passing the legislation required before the beginning of the following week—an interval of two working days— it was considered advisable to endeavour to steady the market and to check the tendency towards a rise in exchange rates. With this object, tenders were invited for the sale to Government of a telegraphic transfer on London to the amount of £100,000. A few tentative bids were made, but none was accepted. The hint appeared to have been sufficient, and to have had the desired effect of stopping further speculative transactions.

This procedure led to some very hostile criticism on the part of the *Straits Times*, which unjustly accused the Government of endeavouring deliberately to get a better rate from the Banks, knowing in advance that the fixed rate would be lower than the Bank rate then prevailing.

On the 29th January, 1906, Ordinance I. of 1906, which enabled the Currency Commissioners to give out notes in exchange for gold locally and against telegraphic transfers in favour of the Crown Agents for the Colonies in London, was passed at one sitting of the Legislative Council, and on the same day an Order of the Governor in Council was passed authorising the Commissioners to receive gold in exchange for notes at the rate of £7 to $60.

On this day the spot price of standard silver was 2/6¼ per ounce, and the corresponding value of the silver content of the dollar was 2/1⅛. For the price of the silver content of the Straits dollar to reach

the value of 2/4, the spot price of bar silver would
have to be $2/9\frac{3}{16}$ per ounce, so that when the
dollar was fixed a margin of safety of about ten per
cent. was provided below the bullion par of $33/\frac{3}{16}$ of
the Straits dollar.

It must be admitted that the plan of not
announcing in advance, as was done in India, the
exchange value of the dollar to be fixed, did not
achieve the object of preventing speculation; but
the chief reason for adopting the cautious policy of
controlling the supply of the dollar, and then being
guided by experience as to the determination of the
value to be given to it, is to be found in the policy
adopted by the Straits Settlements Currency
Committee of giving the people the currency they
wanted, and of avoiding disturbance of trade and of
contracts by making the exchange value to be fixed
as close as possible to the market rate of the day.
These were considered to be the essential features of
the scheme. To make the new dollar readily
acceptable, it had to conform in weight, fineness,
and shape to the old dollar, and to prevent
dislocation of business and hardship between
creditor and debtor, the fixed value had to be
approximately the market rate ruling at the time of
fixing.

This procedure has been the subject of much
criticism. It is commented on as follows in one of
these criticisms :—

" The weight and fineness of the dollar, once
decided upon, seems to have been assumed to be

unalterable. The silver content of the dollar was the fixed thing, so the Currency Committee appear to have reasoned; the unit of value was the alterable thing. This was to be adjusted to the coin and to be fixed at such a rate as to allow a safe margin above bullion value. But one would, naturally ask, why not reverse the procedure? The bullion value of token coins is largely a question of convenience. . . . . The unit of value, on the other hand, is of the utmost importance. Alterations in the unit of value by their uneven effects on the prices of various classes of commodities, upon wages, and by the derangements they cause in the relations existing between debtor and creditor, profoundly affect the whole economic structure. Variations in the value of precious metals have frequently compelled countries to alter the weight and fineness of their coins. Within a short time Japan, Mexico, and the Philippines have taken measures in this direction, consequent on the recent high price of silver. The Straits Settlements, however, afford the only instance in recent monetary history of a material alteration in the unit of value, deliberately made to meet such a contingency."[*]

This was written before the further rise in the price of silver compelled the Government of the Straits Settlements to reduce the weight of their coins. It may be asked what was the unit of value which existed in the Straits Settlements before fixity,

[*] "A Gold Standard for the Straits Settlements," by E. W. Kemmerer.

and what was the material alteration made. The exchange value of the dollar fluctuated with the price of silver, and depended on the silver content of the dollar. The local value of the dollar, so far as the majority of the trading community was concerned, was also measured by the value of the silver contained in the dollar. When these dollars found their way into the interior of China, they were dealt with as sycee, viz., weighed and tested and accepted at the value of their pure silver content. There being no permanent unit of value, it cannot be said that there was any material alteration in the value of the unit when the dollar was fixed at 2/4. If any one will take the trouble to compare the fluctuations in the exchange of the dollar during the twenty years preceding fixity, he cannot escape the conclusion that 2/4 was a much fairer average than the 2/- value which the community and the Government first desired to fix the dollar at. In the Straits Settlements the value of the dollar was fixed below the rate at which it was then circulating. It is contended that it should have been fixed at the rate at which it circulated when these dollars were first made legal tender in 1903, and to prevent their exportation for sale as bullion the silver content of the dollar should have been immediately reduced. The writer* goes on to say that, whereas in other countries a practically existing unit was assumed which would, henceforth, be a fixed unit for the entire currency system, and all

* Dr. G. Visseringh, Chinese Currency.

the coins in circulation were all made subordinate to this unit, and although in British India the existing silver rupee was taken as the unit, and in the Straits dollar the existing dollar (since 1903 the Straits dollar), they were not accepted at the value at which they were then circulating. The procedure indicated as the proper method rests on the assumption that no more violent fluctuations would take place from the date of the selection of the value of the unit and the date when a sufficiency of the new currency would be available to displace the existing currency. According to this plan, the selected value would have been of no use if the market value of the dollar, when the new supply was ready, had diverged considerably from the market value obtaining where the unit was chosen. The essential feature of the scheme suggested by these critics is, that there would have been no delay and no period of uncertainty intervening sufficient to dislocate trade and derange prices. Let us see how this plan would have worked out in 1903-1904, taking three months as the shortest time required for coining the dollars and putting them into circulation. I will take the Hong-Kong rates of exchange, as there was no artificial contraction of the currency in that Colony. In November, 1903, the lowest Hong-Kong rate was $20\frac{7}{8}$; it went still lower in December. Suppose, then, that the unit of value was fixed at 21d. and orders were given for the coinage of dollars adjusted to that value for delivery in February. In February, according to the foregoing criticisms, the authorities would have been able to put these dollars into circulation at the fixed rate, without any dislocation of prices. But, in February, the dollar had gone up to 23¼d., and the plan of bringing in a dollar at a unit of value as close as possible to the existing market rate would have been defeated.

It is asserted, with a good deal of confidence, that the bullion content of the unit of value is a matter of comparative indifference, so long as the coin is convenient to handle, does not unduly encourage counterfeiting and is not so large as to endanger its being melted down. This may be true when once the value of the unit has been completely dissociated from the value of the silver content of the coin representing it, and when the public have thoroughly recognised the fact that it is only a token; but the authorities in the Straits Settlements had to deal with a public which, for a very considerable period of years, have looked on the value of their standard coin as the value of the metal contained in it. The value of the standard coin had not only fluctuated iu relation to articles produced in gold-using countries, but its value, as measured locally, was reflected in the increased prices of local articles and in the increased wages of native employees.

The Dutch Colony of Sumatra and the Malayan States of Siam have provided us with an object lesson in this matter. In Sumatra, there is a large alien population of Chinese—petty traders and coolies. Although the official accounts and those of many of the mercantile firms and estates were kept in Dutch currency, the coins in circulation were the dollars in use in the Straits Settlements. Though the project of demonetising these dollars and of replacing them with the Dutch guilder had long been in contemplation, the Netherlands-Indian Government did not succeed in getting their currency generally accepted until some time after the Straits Settlements Government had reformed the currency and completed the coinage of their new and smaller dollar. The situation in Sumatra was similar to that in the Straits Settlements when the East India Company made their unsuccessful efforts to force the rupee into circulation as the standard coin. The same experience befell the the Siamese Government, in the Siamese Malay States, when they attempted to put their own ticels in circulation in place of the dollars used in the Straits Settlements which were current there to the exclusion of Siamese coins. They succeeded only after the Straits Settlements had introduced their currency scheme and restricted the currency area of the Straits dollar.

The history of the currency reforms in the Philippines also shows that what were rightly considered to be the fundamental requirements in the Straits Settlements Currency scheme, viz., that the size and fineness of the existing standard should be adhered to, and that the value of the standard should be as nearly as possible the market rate then prevailing, were carefully observed. When the currency of the Philippines was transferred from a silver to a gold basis, the new Philippine peso introduced was 416 grains and 900 fineness, the same as the British and the first Straits dollars, and to make the value of the unit conform as closely as possible consistently with safety with the market rate of the coin, a coinage ratio of 32·25 to 1 was adopted. This gave a bullion par of 29¼d. per ounce, and provided a considerably smaller margin of safety than the Straits dollar. The procedure, in all essentials excepting that of contracting the currency and being guided by the further experience gained, was the same as that in the Straits Settlements. The reform took two years to complete, as against two and a half years in the Straits Settlements, and the bullion par being less, the Philippines peso stood in much greater danger of the melting pot than the Straits dollar. The coinage ratio which, it was hoped, would effect, by means of an international agreement, the object of limiting the fluctuations of silver within certain points had to be abandoned, and was made the alterable quantity.

It was thought, in some quarters, that because the Straits public had readily accepted notes, they would have been as ready to accept a lighter weight dollar even before a definite gold value had been given to that coin. It is true that the great majority of the business men in the Colony had great belief in the general acquiescence of the public in a Government issue of one-dollar notes. The

popularity of the Bank-note issues in the Colony
and the Federated Malay States, and the prevalence
in all the more important towns of the system of
chits, which were accepted by petty traders,
hawkers, hackney carriage drivers, and even by
rikisha pullers from known residents, were sufficient
grounds for this belief; but I think that the
consensus of opinion on the part of the mercantile
community was against the theory that a lighter
weight coin would be accepted as a final payment.
At any rate, a large majority of the merchants who
were called as witnesses before the Straits Settlements Currency Committee held a different view,
and their evidence goes to show that they were of
the opinion that the most essential feature of the
currency scheme was the substitution for the
existing trade dollar of a Government dollar of the
same size and fineness. Those who believe that a
lighter coin would have been readily accepted
point to the fact that the new and smaller Straits
dollar, made legal tender in 1907, was quietly
accepted throughout the country. It must be borne
in mind that the conditions were then totally different.
The one-dollar note had by then largely displaced
the dollar; it had become known that these notes
were accepted in Hong-Kong and at the Treaty
Ports at a rate based on the sterling rate of 2/4, and
commanded a higher value than the British or
Mexican dollar; that the sovereign could be obtained
at a slight premium over the fixed rate, and at par
from the Currency Commissioners, when gold was

available, and that sterling Bank drafts, rupee Bank drafts and drafts on China and Java were based on this rate. To what extent the note had displaced the dollar may be seen from the fact that the coinage of the first Straits dollar amounted to $35,400,576, whilst the total number of the new and lighter Straits dollars and the fifty cent. pieces minted was only $19,006,872. Over twelve millions of these has been held in the currency note reserve and is still so held, leaving less than seven millions in active circulation, in the Banks and Government Treasuries.

It will be seen, therefore, that the popularity of the one dollar note and its known exchange value made the silver content of the dollar a matter of comparative indifference to the community. Another argument in favour of the opinion, that the lighter dollar would not have been willingly accepted at the beginning, can be seen in the fact that the fifty cent. piece, though made a full legal tender coin, never became a popular coin. When it was made an unlimited legal tender coin at the end of 1906, it was expected that, owing to its convenient size, it would soon get into favour with the general public, and the authorities entertained the hope that it would make it possible to retire altogether the more cumbrous coin. However, there was no greater demand for it than before, and some portion of these coins had afterwards to be sold as bullion.

Another criticism, often heard during the course

of our currency changes, was that we should have waited for silver to decline in value before fixing the dollar, and that the method, followed in India, where the value of the rupee was fixed during a falling market in silver, should have been followed in the Straits Settlements. The only advantage from a falling market in silver in connection with their currency changes was that, with the control over the supply of dollars in Government's hands, a sure indication of the dissociation of the dollar from silver would have been afforded, if the dollar had maintained its exchange value and did not decline in value with every fall in the price of silver. To have fixed the dollar at a low rate when silver was low would have been to lull ourselves into a false sense of security. That India carried out her currency changes during a period of declining silver was largely a matter of circumstances and not of deliberate policy. It could not have been foreseen. In fact, the conditions in Iudia were very unfavourable for the establishment of a gold standard, and it took five years before Indian exchange reached the declared value of 1/4, owing to the low price of silver and the excessive amount of rupees in circulation. Attempts were made by the Indian Government to force exchange up to 1/4 by withholding the sale of Council Bills, but they proved unsuccessful, and were given up. It may be here remarked that the Indian Government, in fixing the rupee at 1/4, provided a very good margin between the bullion par and the value of the silver content of the rupee as prices then ruled, and it will be seen that India was the only country in the East, which had adopted a gold exchange standard, which was not compelled to recoin its standard coinage by reason of the rise in the price of silver.

This summary covers the operations up to the date of the fixing of the dollar at 2/4. I have endeavoured, in addition, to give the reasons, as they appear to me, for the measures undertaken by the Government in pursuance of the recommendations of the Straits Settlements Currency Committee, and to reply to some of the criticisms urged against them. The important changes made in the scheme, in consequence of the further rise in the price of silver, deserve a separate chapter.

CHAPTER II

EFFECT OF THE RISE IN THE PRICE OF SILVER ON THE CURRENCY SYSTEM

IN January, 1905, when the dollar was fixed at 2/4, the maximum spot price of bar silver was 30¼. The value of the silver content of the dollar at this rate was 2/1⅛ and its bullion par $33\frac{3}{16}$, thus giving a margin of safety of about 10 per cent. With a few set-backs, silver continued to rise until it reached the maximum of 33⅛ per oz. of standard silver.

The following table gives the maximum spot price of standard silver for each month of the year and the corresponding value of the silver content of the dollar. The expenses in connection with the sale of the dollars as bullion should be taken into account. They consist of the cost of transport (freight, insurance, packing, and dock charges) and the cost of melting and refining to standard fineness. An allowance of $1\frac{5}{16}$ per cent. will probably cover all these costs. The margin of safety, therefore, is in reality greater than that shown in this table :—

1906		Maximum spot price of bar silver.	Value of the silver content of the dollar.
January	...	$30\frac{1}{4}$	$2/1\frac{1}{8}$
February	...	$30\frac{13}{16}$	$2/1\frac{5}{8}$
March ...	...	$30\frac{5}{8}$	$2/1\frac{7}{16}$
April ...	...	$30\frac{9}{16}$	$2/1\frac{3}{8}$
May ...	...	$31\frac{5}{16}$	$2/2\frac{9}{16}$
June ...	...	$31\frac{1}{8}$	$2/1\frac{7}{8}$
July ...	...	$30\frac{5}{16}$	$2/1\frac{9}{16}$
August...	...	$30\frac{15}{16}$	$2/1\frac{11}{16}$
September	...	$31\frac{3}{4}$	$2/2\frac{3}{8}$
October	...	$32\frac{9}{16}$	$2/3\frac{1}{16}$
November	...	$33\frac{1}{8}$	$2/3\frac{9}{16}$
December	...	$32\frac{3}{8}$	$2/2\frac{7}{8}$

It will be seen that the margin of safety of 10 per cent. provided at the beginning had dwindled down to 2 per cent., and the dollars were, therefore, dangerously near the point where it would be profitable to export them for sale as bullion. The Government were accordingly again confronted with the problem of providing a sufficient margin of safety between the fixed value and the melting-down point of the dollar.

Two courses were open to them. One was to leave the size and fineness of the dollar as it was, and to raise its gold value to, say, 2/6; the other was to leave the value of the dollar at the rate it was fixed at in January, and to debase the dollar.

The criticisms, to which I referred in the preceding chapter as to the method adopted for fixing the dollar, now applied with a great deal of force and justice to the first course. The dollar was now a proper unit of value. It had a stable exchange value which the public were led to believe would prove unalterable. Exchange had maintained its stability since fixity for a period of eleven months. Mercantile transactions had been conducted on the basis of a stable exchange without the cover formerly necessary against frequent fluctuations. In the relations between debtor and creditor no allowances were continued to be made for frequent fluctuations of exchange. The Government and all other large employers had based the salaries of their employees on the fixed value of the dollar. The alteration of the value of the unit would have meant the reconsideration of most long term contracts, an increase for some time in the working expenses of every industry worked with gold capital, and a depreciation of the dollar value of all the sterling investments which people had been induced to put their money into by the prospect of a stable currency. The loss, especially to the Currency

E

Commissioners, would have been very great by the depreciation in the dollar value of their sterling investments and their gold reserves, and the liability imposed by statute to make good this deficiency out of the general revenue of the Colony would have seriously embarrassed the Colony.

On the other hand, circumstances were very favourable for bringing in a smaller standard coin. The note with its known exchange value had displaced the dollar to a large extent, and it was known that a very much smaller amount of dollars would be sufficient for the purposes of circulation. There is no need to recapitulate the reasons already given in the previous chapter in dealing with the criticisms of the recommendations of the Straits Settlements Currency Committee (see pages 36-42). The Government, therefore, had no hesitation in adopting the course of adhering to the fixed value, and of reducing the bullion value of the dollar. Before any decision was arrived at as to the weight and fineness of the new dollar, preparations were made for shipping the dollars in the currency coin reserve for reminting, and for drawing in the existing dollars in the Banks and the possession of the public by the issue of $1 notes. Additional measures were considered advisable in view of a possible stringency of coin. Sovereigns were made legal tender. The legal tender of the fifty cent piece and of the one dollar note, which was limited to ten dollars, was made unlimited.

The first proposal of the Government was the

reduction of the fineness of the Straits dollar to 800, keeping the weight and size intact, and an order of the King-in-Council was issued on the 22nd October, 1906, making the sovereign legal tender in the Colony, substituting a dollar of 800 fineness instead of 900 as the standard, and making the Straits Settlements' fifty cent piece legal tender for any amount. An Ordinance (xxvi. of 1906), was also passed, and came into operation on the same date, making it lawful for the Currency Commissioners to require a person, when presenting notes, to accept such current coin as they may tender, excepting subsidiary coin in excess of the sum for which such subsidiary coin was legal tender. The Ordinance also provided that from such date as shall be notified by the Governor-in-Council, by publication in the " Gazette," a person may be required, when presenting notes, to accept their equivalent in gold at the fixed rate.

It may be noticed here that Ordinance xxii. of 1906, which was passed on the 14th September, whereby the Currency Commissioners were empowered to sell at the gold export point telegraphic transfers payable by the Crown Agents in London, with the object of fixing a downward limit to the exchange value of the dollar, incidentally tended to sustain the confidence of the public in the adequacy of the machinery at the disposal of Government for preventing any undue depletion of the local coin reserves. It tended to relieve the pressure on these reserves by enabling the Currency

Commissioners to accept notes in exchange for gold given out in London.

When the proposal of the Straits Government to reduce the dollar was submitted to the home authorities, the question of adopting the alternative course of withdrawing the order in Council fixing the rate of exchange at $60 to £7, setting the dollar free to rise in value as silver rises, and of taking the opportunity to carry the dollar to a higher point later on, was again discussed and rejected, on the ground of the dislocation of business which would be entailed during the transition period, and the great importance of pressing on the public the conviction that the dollar had now a definite gold value. Silver reached $33\frac{1}{8}$ in November, 1906, and it was evident that the margin of safety with a dollar of 800 fineness, but of the same weight as the existing dollar, would be insufficient. The bullion par of such a dollar would be $37\frac{5}{16}$.

The question for decision now lay between the two following proposals :—

Reduction of weight to 312 grains, and reduction of fineness to 800.

Reduction of weight to 312 grains, but no reduction in fineness.

The bullion par, viz., for the price of silver in these dollars to reach the limit of 2/4 (without making any allowance for shipment, melting, and refining, &c., which would probably amount to $1\frac{15}{16}$ per cent.), would be in the first case $49\frac{13}{16}$d., and in the second $44\frac{1}{4}$d.

The opinion of the Lords Commissioners of the Treasury was that the first proposal appeared to provide for a reduction of the dollar beyond what was reasonably necessary, and that a reduction of the weight to 312 grains was all that was necessary, as silver would have to reach a price of over 44d. before a dollar of 900 fineness and 312 grains would touch melting point. It was pointed out that the retention of the 900 fineness would greatly facilitate recoinage, and that the Mint charges would be appreciably less.

The representatives of public opinion, the Chambers of Commerce, &c., were consulted in the matter, and declared in favour of retaining the fineness. The Chinese Chamber of Commerce and the Advisory Board especially were strongly opposed to reducing the fineness of the dollar, and the Legislative Council unanimously voted in favour of retaining the 900 fineness and reducing the weight to 312 grains.

The protection afforded by this reduction would appear to be ample. The bullion par of $44\frac{1}{4}$d. gives a coinage ratio of 21.3 to 1, the same as that of the new Philippine peso, and is below that of the Indian rupee with its ratio of 21.9 to 1, and the Japanese half-yen with its ratio of 21.6 to 1. The outer fortification of the Indian rupee and the Japanese silver half-yen must be taken first before the Straits Settlements new dollar could be seized for sale as bullion. The effect of any wholesale sale of Indian rupees on the silver market could readily be imagined.

India, having provided herself with a sufficiently large margin, the rise in the price of silver had no effect on its currency; but it is interesting to note that in the two countries where the method followed was first fixing on a unit of value, and then adjusting the silver content of their standard coin to this unit, the authorities were compelled to recoin their currency by the rise in silver. The Philippine peso was reduced from 416 grains and 900 fineness to 309 grains and 800 fineness, which meant a change in the coinage ratio from 32.25 to 1 to 21.3 to 1. The Japanese silver half-yen was reduced from 166.375 grains to 125 grains, the coinage ratio being changed from 28.75 to 1 to 21.6 to 1.

The question is often asked, what should the Government do in case silver rose above 44¼d., and the dollars were in danger of being melted down for sale as bullion. I am convinced that the proper solution would be to leave the silver dollars to their fate and to let gold come in to take their place, not as a circulating medium but as a backing for the notes. It is unnecessary and wasteful to have two forms of currency for the same denomination of value circulating side by side, and experience has proved that the dollar note is better adapted as a circulating medium than the dollar, and is now more readily accepted. Notes and subsidiary coin, with a sufficiently strong gold backing, will satisfactorily meet the currency requirements of the Colony and the Federated Malay States. The question why gold should only be used to form the reserve, and not as a circulating medium, will be dealt with later on.

The weight and fineness of the dollar having been decided upon, it was considered advisable to make the fifty cent piece exactly half the weight of the new dollar, with the same fineness, and to sell as bullion all the fifty cent pieces as soon as the recoinage was completed. An order of the King-in-Council was passed in February, 1907, for the coinage of these new dollars and fifty cent pieces.

The recoinage was completed early in 1909. The total number of new dollars and fifty cent pieces received was $19,006,872, which gave a surplus of $4,751,898 over the amount sent for reminting. This sum was credited at its bullion value to the Gold Standard Reserve established by Ordinance iii. of 1905. Out of the amount of $19,006,872, about twelve and a half millions were received into the coin reserve of the note issue. In addition to this, there was left in the reserve a balance of over $9,600,000 old Straits dollars. It was decided to sell this as bullion as soon as circumstances became favourable. $3,00,000 old Straits dollars had already been sold in 1907 at a favourable price. The sale of the balance was completed in 1911, and a substantial gold reserve of well over £1,000,000 was established in London, half of which was kept in actual coin and half in money at short notice, Treasury bills and money at call with certain banks approved by the Secretary of State.

It will be seen, then, that the rise in the price of

silver, which was at the time regarded as a calamity by the whole of the community, inasmuch as it prevented the Government from giving an exchange value of 2/- to the dollar, and compelled them to adopt a unit of value which was considered much too high, and, therefore, likely to affect injuriously all local industries, has proved to be a blessing in disguise.   It has placed the currency scheme on a secure footing by means of the effective gold reserve it has enabled the Government to accumulate in London.

CHAPTER III

GOLD LEGAL TENDER

ALTHOUGH gold was eventually made legal tender in the Straits Settlements, this action was only permitted by the home authorities solely with the object of coping with the possible danger of a large demand for metallic currency during the depletion of the silver reserve by its being sent abroad for recoinage. With reference to this question, the Straits Settlements Currency Committee held the view that it would not be indispensable that gold coins should be made legal tender in the Colony and the States after the establishment of the gold standard. The system they desired to introduce was that of an over-valued silver coin as a circulating medium, with gold to be paid into a reserve or taken out of it for satisfying international trade requirements, and they evidently were of the opinion that there was no necessity for the use of gold as a circulating medium.

The principle of this system is the same as that elucidated by Ricardo in his book, " The Principles of Political Economy and Taxation," chapter xxvii. There he states : " To secure the public against any other variations in the value of currency than those to which the standard itself is subject, and, at the same time, to carry on the circulation with a medium the least expensive is to attain the most perfect state to which a currency can be brought, and we should possess all these advantages by subjecting the Bank to the delivery of uncoined gold at the Mint standard and price in exchange for their notes, instead of the delivery of guineas, by which means paper would never fall below the value of bullion without being followed by a reduction of its quantity. To prevent the rise of paper above the value of bullion, the Bank should be also obliged to give their paper in exchange for standard gold at the price of £3 17s. per ounce. Not to give too much trouble to the Bank, the quantity of gold to be demanded in exchange for paper at the Mint price of £3 17s. 10½d., or the quantity to be sold to the Bank at £3 17s., should never be less than twenty ounces. In other words, the Bank should be obliged to purchase any quantity of gold that was offered them not less than twenty ounces at £3 17s. per ounce, and to sell any quantity that might be demanded at £3 17s. 10½d., and while they have the power of regulating the quantity of their paper, there is no possible inconvenience that could result to them from such an arrangement.

" *The most perfect liberty should be given at the same time to import or export every description of bullion.* These transactions would be very few in number if the Banks regulated their loans and issues of paper by the criterion which I have so often mentioned, viz., the price of standard bullion without attending to the absolute quantity of paper in circulation."

In a footnote he adds that the price of £3 17s. here mentioned was an arbitrary price. There might be good reason for fixing it a little above or a little below, and in naming £3 17s. he wished only to elucidate the principle. *The price ought to be so fixed as to make it the interest of the seller of gold rather to sell it to the Bank than to carry it to the Mint to be coined.* The same remark applied to the specified quantity of twenty ounces. There might be good reason for making it ten or thirty.

John Stuart Mill, in his "Principles of Political Economy," expressed a similar view. "A country with the extensive commercial relations of England is liable suddenly to be called upon for large foreign payments, sometimes in loans or other investments of capital abroad, sometimes as the price of some unusual importations of goods, the most frequent case being that of large importations of food consequent on a bad harvest. To meet such demands it is necessary that there should be either in circulation, or in the coffers of the banks, coin or bullion to a very considerable amount, and that this, when drawn out by any emergency, should be allowed to return after the emergency is past. But since gold wanted for exportation is almost invariably drawn from the reserves of the banks, and is never likely to be taken directly from the circulation while the banks remain solvent, *the only advantage which can be obtained from retaining partially a metallic currency for daily purpose is, that the banks may occasionally replenish their reserves from it "* (Book III., chapter xxii.).

The question of making gold legal tender was raised long before the necessity arose in consequence of the depletion of the silver reserves from their being shipped abroad for recoinage. The arguments used in favour of this action may be summed up as follows :—

That in the large towns of the Peninsula a gold currency would prove very convenient, and would be largely used ; it would be easier at any time to limit the amount for which the dollar was legal tender, and to replace the existing stock with dollars of less fineness and content; that it would render it unnecessary to add to the existing stock of dollars for many years to come, as any required expansion of the currency could be met by gold or by the issue of notes against gold ; the extremely cumbrous nature of the existing currency was a constant annoyance to the large and growing European population, and the large well-to-do Chinese and other nationalities, and that the growth of the note issue, before the issue of the one-dollar note, pointed to a demand for a convenient medium of high value like gold; the great object of making gold legal tender was to impress the public, especially the Chinese, who are so conservative, with the fact that the essence of the Government's action in regard to the currency has been to change the dollar from a silver dollar to a definite fraction of a sovereign, and that, when once gold is made legal tender, the public would soon come to realise that it was the real standard; that so long as the obligation to redeem our notes in silver dollars remained, it would be difficult to disabuse the minds of our population of the idea that the value of the dollar depended on its silver content, and not on the fact that it commanded a definite value in gold.

The objections against sovereigns being made legal tender were, that gold was scarcely suitable for circulation in an Eastern country where the needs of the community are sufficiently met by a silver coinage and currency notes; the expense of the sovereign was considerable, and fell on the British taxpayer at home; there was no evidence to show that gold would be suitable as a circulating medium in the Malay Peninsula; it would be more prudent to hold all the gold that comes into the hands of Government as security for the gold value of the dollar; making sovereigns legal tender would only operate to prevent a drain of dollars from the Colony (in case the bullion value of the dollar rose appreciably above the fixed value) so far as the holdings of the Currency Commissioners were concerned, and, then only if the Commissioners were empowered to refuse silver in exchange for notes, and, as the notes were originally issued in exchange for silver dollars, the refusal to cash them in silver would not be a justifiable measure; gold in circulation could not be readily utilised for meeting international payments; it would be more convenient that the gold required for this purpose should not be in circulation, but collected at a central institution such as the Currency Commissioners' Reserve, from which it could be drawn out for export when the requirements of trade demanded it.

Owing to the ratio fixed between the dollar and sovereign, the latter became an inconvenient and unsuitable coin to use for circulating purposes in the Colony, and gold was thereby prevented from becoming scattered and being rendered unavailable for the purpose of meeting international payments. There is no need, therefore, to regret the impracticability of turning the sovereign into a circulating medium in the Colony and the States, especially as it is the interest of the Government not to do anything to encourage its circulation.   It will be seen, then, that the Colony is again indebted to the rise in the price of silver which, by compelling the Government to fix the dollar at a ratio that rendered the sovereign unsuitable for circulation, conferred a distinct benefit on the Colony by enabling the Government to accumulate gold at centres whence it could be readily drawn for the purpose of foreign remittances.

CHAPTER IV

THIS record will not be complete without some account of the part assigned to the subsidiary coin in the currency scheme and the measures taken to obtain a clean currency of subsidiary coins entirely under the control of the Government.

It must be admitted that a good deal of the Straits subsidiary coin was coined by the Straits Government and the States of Perak and Selangor for the purpose of obtaining revenue, without careful regard to the internal requirements of these countries. Much of it was taken abroad, chiefly to China. The Straits Settlements Currency Committee did not anticipate any serious trouble from this cause. They considered that if these coins were returned and put into circulation in such quantities as did not cause the coins to fall below their face value no harm would be done; if they fell below the face value, the tendency of such coins to be returned would be checked, and that, under the most unfavourable circumstances, the difficulty would be met by the Straits Government withdrawing a portion of this coinage.

As soon as Government, however, took steps to have a dollar of their own, Chinese speculators set to work to collect these coins in China and to import them into the Straits. The Government arranged to take a definite amount from them every month and to redeem them in dollars. This arrangement continued for several years, and was not finally concluded till 1908.

Arrangements were also made through the Banks to take over the surplus coins from the principal firms whose dealings necessitated the acceptance of payments in small coin. The opium and spirit farmer was allowed to pay $15,000 a month of his rent in small coin, and the collections of the tramway company, and the market farmers also found their way into the local Treasury.

These arrangements prevented the small coin from going to a greater discount than two per mille below their face value, but the result was that a large part of the Government income was held in a form that was unrealizable. At the end of the year 1906 the subsidiary coinage withdrawn from circulations amounted to $1,052,329, and by the end of 1912 a total of $3,624,523 had been withdrawn, of which $2,071,353 was reminted into the new subsidiary coin of 600 fineness, and the balance was sold. There was still estimated to be nearly $4,000,000 old subsidiary coin in circulation at the end of 1913.

The reduction of the dollar from 416 grains to 312 grains made it necessary to reduce either the weight or the fineness or both of subsidiary coins. It was found impracticable to reduce the weight as the smallest silver current, the five cent pieces which was about the size of the English threepence, could not be further reduced in size. The fineness of these coins was accordingly reduced to 600 from 800. The silver content of a dollar's worth of these new coins is not far below that of the new Straits dollar.

It has been seen that during the withdrawal of dollars from Singapore for recoinage, the 50 cent piece was made full legal tender to meet any demands that might have arisen for silver currency in exchange for notes. The suggestion was also made that the legal tender of the subsidiary coin should be raised from two dollars to twenty dollars. It would have proved a great convenience to the public, and would have, at that time, relieved the market to a considerable extent. The suggestion was not acted upon, but it seems to be worth reconsideration. The present limit is much too low. The effect of raising their legal tender will, to some extent, increase the volume of currency, but I think there is more room for an increase in this department than of the full legal tender silver.

The fifty cent piece, having been raised to a full legal tender status, was recoined, and is now of the same fineness as the dollar and exactly half the weight. It can now be held in the coin reserve to

F

secure the convertibility of the note. The other subsidiary coins, although their silver content is approximately equivalent, in proportion to their value, to the silver content of the dollar and the half-dollar, are not permitted to be held as a reserve against the note issue, although the dollar and the half-dollar are now no less token coins than the subsidiary coins. Though the note is only a promise to pay in dollars, there is in public belief a definite gold value attached to it, and the dollar and the half-dollar will not go much further towards the redemption of the note than the rest of the subsidiary silver coin. The inconvenience to trade occasioned by the surplus small coin returned from China has been overcome, and the question of hoarding it against the issue of notes is not likely to arise again. If these coins are not allowed to be held in the reserve, there does not seem to be much object in endeavouring to cover the difference between their token value in gold and their bullion value by holding specie or securities.

As regards copper coin, the Governments of British North Borneo and Sarawak had for a considerable period inundated the Colony and the Federated Malay States with their issues of copper cents, which were exactly of the same size and weight as the copper cent of the Straits Settlements. The profits from this source yielded a considerable revenue to these Governments.

The effects of allowing these coins to circulate side by side with the Straits copper cents was to

depreciate the value of the latter coin, and, owing to
the considerable quantities current in the market,
it was found difficult to dispose of the large collec-
tions of copper coins which came into the possession
of rice dealers and the Tramway Company, &c., for
dollars except at a very heavy discount.

The circulation of the Sarawak copper coins,
being small in comparison with that of the British
North Borneo cents, the prohibition of their
importation and circulation was dealt with first.
The latter step was taken in 1901, but not until
after the Government had bought up all the
Sarawak copper coin which could be found and
returned it to the Sarawak Government, which took
it over.

In 1906, the British North Borneo copper coin in
circulation was estimated to be not less than 25
per cent. of the total copper coin in circulation.
The order prohibiting the importation of these
coins into the Colony had not been very effective, it
having been very difficult, owing to the absence of
customs regulations, to prevent their importation
even in large quantities. Measures were taken in
1907 to stop the circulation of these coins before
bringing into effect the order to prohibit their
currency. Notices were issued that Straits cents
would be given in exchange for British North
Borneo up to the end of the year, and a sufficient
supply of Straits copper coins was ordered from
the Mint. Of the British North Borneo coins
received in exchange, the Government of that

country were persuaded to take back in their copper
coin a portion of a debt due to them from the Straits
Settlements; a part of it was recoined into Straits
cents and the remainder sold to the Calcutta Mint.

Thus, by the end of 1908, the whole of the
currency of the Colony and the Malay States came
under the direct control of the Government of the
Straits Settlements, and no expansion of currency
was possible except on the initiative of Government
or by the tender of gold by the public.

There is one point worth noting before proceeding
to the next part of this chapter, and that is the
gradual disappearance from the markets of the
principal towns of the half-cent and the quarter-cent
pieces. These coins were very much in evidence in
the seventies and eighties, and a good deal of small
business was done through their medium in the
bazaars. With the depreciation in the exchange
value of the dollar, which reached its lowest limit in
the early nineties, they gradually grew less and less
until they have almost disappeared. The half-cent
piece is occasionally seen, but the quarter-cent very
rarely. The former are used only at the docks for
tallying coal cargoes.

The statement is frequently made, and I believe a
portion of the public credit it, that the value of the
dollar, notwithstanding the numerous fluctations in
its exchange value, has not appreciably altered in
relation to local commodities. The use of the half-
cent and the quarter-cent piece was entirely
restricted to local commodities, and the disappear-

ance of these coins is to me a very significant proof of the general rise in the price of all local commodities, caused not least of all by a depreciating currency in terms of which such price was measured.

The question of having a collateral currency for the use of the native traders from the neighbouring countries, who would wish to take part of the proceeds of the sale of their produce in the Colony home with them in the form of cash, and not in commodities, was prominently brought before the Straits Settlements Currency Committee by one of its members, and great importance was attached to it by some of the witnesses. In this matter the Committee made the following observations :—

" It has been represented to us that the trade of the Straits Settlements is accompanied and facilitated by a large import and re-export of silver dollars, and it is feared that that trade might be injured if either the import of Mexican and British dollars were prohibited, or if Mexican and British dollars ceased to be legal currency. As regards this matter, we desire to point out that the prohibition of the import of Mexican and British dollars would only be a temporary measure, and that simultaneously the exchange of the new special Straits dollar for the existing currency would provide a supply of Mexican and British dollars more than sufficient to meet the wants of trade, while after the completion of the exchange, and on the demonetization of the British and Mexican dollar, the prohibition of importation would be withdrawn, and Mexican and

British dollars might continue to be imported and exported as merchandise in any quantities that the trade of the Straits Settlements might require.   To allay possible apprehension, however, it might be well to provide, when the general import of Mexican and British dollars is prohibited, that such dollars might be imported *for purposes of re-export,* with the sanction in each case of the Straits Government and on such conditions as that Government might, prescribe."

The first special Straits dollar was coined in sufficient quantities to take the place of the British and Mexican dollars current in Sumatra, the Siamese Malay States, and other countries outside the jurisdiction of the British Government.   No necessity, therefore, arose for the withdrawal of the order of 1903, prohibiting the importation of Mexican and British dollars into the Colony and the Federated Malay States.   As regards China, in addition to the facilities given by the Banks and private Chinese firms which conducted a remittance business, the Straits notes were freely made use of in place of dollars for carrying savings into China by the more intelligent Chinese who had no difficulty in Hong Kong and the treaty ports, in exchanging them into local currency at nearly their proper value.

It was not till 1907, however, after measures were taken to introduce the second and smaller special Straits dollar, that it was pointed out that some hardship might be experienced by ignorant coolies returning to China with their savings when the new dollar became current. It was, therefore, proposed that facilities should be given in the Straits Settlements for exchanging these new dollars for dollars current in Hong Kong and China, and that the prohibition of the importation of British and Mexican dollars should be withdrawn.

A withdrawal of the order was not considered advisable, owing to the replacement of the first Straits dollars by pieces of less weight, then proceeding, and of the temptation to pass into circulation full-weight British or Mexican dollars in place of the lighter coin of higher gold value, and an alternative suggestion was made that the Government should, themselves, import a certain amount of British and Mexican dollars, open bureaux of exchange at the ports of embarkation, and there provide the coolies with dollars for use in China at the current rate of exchange. The coolies would thus be saved from the money-changers, and there would be no interference with legitimate banking business, since the facilities would only be taken advantage of by the ignorant classes carrying their property in cash.

The importance of the object of these measures suggested is obvious. If, owing to the currency changes in the Straits Settlements, the coolies found that they could only exchange their Straits dollars at an appreciable loss, it would have prejudically affected the supply of Chinese labour into the Malay peninsula. The danger seems to have been somewhat exaggerated, and too little faith placed in the sound commercial instincts of the Chinese people.

Owing to the large amount of Mexican and British dollars that would have been required for these transactions, and the possibilities of the Government being involved in speculations in silver, it was decided to extend the money order facilities afforded in the Post Office, instead of establishing bureaux of exchange.

There have been no serious difficulties in the matter of exchange between China and the Straits, and the prohibition of the importation of British and Mexican dollars is still in force and likely to continue. In this respect there has been an important departure from the recommendations of the Straits Settlements Currency Committee.

CHAPTER V

PRIOR to the introduction of the Currency Note Ordinance, 1899, no reserve was kept by the Government against any of the currency issued by them. It has been seen in the foregoing chapters that the Government were only responsible for the subsidiary silver and copper coin, but that the function of supplying the Colony with the standard coin, viz., the Mexican and British dollars, was performed by the Banks established in the Colony. The profits from minting subsidiary silver and copper coin were paid into general revenue, and no special record appears to have been kept either of the amount of such minting or the profits accruing therefrom.

By the Currency Note Ordinance, 1899, the coins received in exchange for notes were paid into a Note Guarantee Fund to secure the convertibility of the note. The principle followed was that the whole of the note issue should be fully covered by coins and securities at their market value, to be maintained in certain proportions. The proportion fixed by this legislation was two-thirds coin and one-third investments, but power was expressly reserved to the

Secretary of State to enable him to vary this proportion and to increase the investment portion to one-half of the Note Guarantee Fund. This power was exercised by him a few years after the passing ·of the Ordinance, so that the Currency Commissioners were given the power to keep a minimum limit of unlimited legal tender coin of one-half, and a maximum investment limit of one-half of the notes in circulation. With a view to maintaining the investments at their cost price level, a sum equivalent to one per cent. of the cost price of the securities had to be paid in annually to a depreciation fund out of the income derived from the investments. The balance, after defraying the annually recurrent cost of the management of the note issue, was paid into general revenue. The general revenue, moreover, was made liable forthwith to make good any deficiency between the cost price and the market value of the securities, as ascertained by the Auditor-General at his annual audit, after taking into account the amount of the depreciation fund. The payment was made by an order of the Governor on the certificate of the Auditor-general, without reference to the Legislative Council or the Finance Committee of the Council, although such payment has, sometimes, been sufficiently large to disturb the expenditure allocated for services authorised in the budget.

Although the securities had, in a few cases, shown some appreciation, the net result was a depreciation which had to be made good in the manner shown above, so that, whilst the Government were taking money annually from the Currency Commissioners for payment into a revenue on which a defence contribution of twenty per cent. was levied, they were obliged to pay back to the Currency Commissioners large lump sums every few years to make good the depreciation of their investments, though no immediate need for such payment existed.

With the introduction of the special Straits dollar, and the closing of the Mint to the coinage of dollars for use in the Straits, the position became still more acute. The securities forming the investment portion of the fund were mainly sterling securities, and, since India had adopted the gold standard, the Indian investments of the Currency Commissioners had become the equivalent of sterling. The dollar value of all these securities fell, as the dollar rose in exchange value. In 1904-1905 it was calculated that the rise by a penny in the exchange value of the dollar meant a further deficiency in the value of the securities, then held by the Currency Commissioners, of well over $200,000. The Currency scheme having been instituted, a continuance of the rise was to be expected until the dollar reached the value at which it was destined to be fixed. The revenue during that time was low, owing to the default of the Opium and Spirit Farmers, and it was seen that the payment of the large sums due to the Currency Commissioners under the Ordinance would have resulted in the curtailment of expenditure on necessary works, and was an unnecessary burden on the resources of the Colony. The Government accordingly made representations to the Secretary of State requesting that the annual payments from the income of the Currency Commissioners investments to general revenue should cease, that the payments from revenue to the Currency Commissioners of the sums certified to be due by the Auditor-General should also cease, and that the whole of the income from investments, after defraying the expenses of management, should be paid to the depreciation fund of the Currency Commissioners. These recommendations were approved (with the exception that the sums certified to be due by the Auditor-General remained a liability of revenue, but their payment was made subject to suspension by the Governor with the sanction of the Secretary of State), and were given effect to in 1905. It should be noted that this measure did not affect the ultimate liability of the revenue of the Colony to make good any insufficiency of cover for the notes in circulation; it provided that no payment from revenue need be made, if, in the opinion of the Governor, it was unnecessary, until such an actual demand should arise as would result in the depletion of the Currency Commissioners' reserves.

In the year, then, prior to the fixing of the dollar in the Colony, the reserves provided by law against the note issue were as follows :—

Coin portion, consisting of legal tender coin, with a minimum limit of one-half of the notes in circulation,

Investment portion, consisting of securities approved by the Secretary of State and Indian Government paper, with a maximum limit of one-half of the notes in circulation, taken at their cost price.

A depreciation fund to which the whole income from investments, less the annually recurrent cost of management, was paid. The whole of this depreciation fund was at first held in permanent securities.

To these was added in the following year by provision in the Currency Note Ordinance, another reserve which was called the Gold Standard Reserve. The principal constituent of this reserve was the profit from minting dollars and subsidiary coin, a matter which lay outside the purview of the Currency Note Ordinance. The other sources from which this reserve was to be fed, viz., the profits from the sale and purchase at specie points of telegraphic transfers and the interest from its investments, were small in comparison with the first source of supply.

Though no change was made in the title of the Ordinance, its character was altered and its scope was enlarged by this innovation. The duty of maintaining the gold par of the dollar was thus thrown on the Currency Commissioners, and the machinery for working it was provided in the Ordinance relating to the Note Issue. At the same time, the distinction, observed in India, between the gold portion of the Paper Currency Reserve and the Gold Standard Reserve was preserved, and, notwithstanding the different conditions in the Straits Settlements, the attempt to follow faithfully the Indian model was persevered in. The gold in the Note Guarantee Fund, we were told, was not to be regarded as an asset of the fund, but only as representing so many dollars at the fixed rate of exchange for the purpose of securing the convertibility of the note; the important point, however, was to secure that the profit obtained by converting gold into Straits dollars should not form part of the Note Guarantee Fund, but should be transferred to a separate gold reserve fund, the formation of which was essential to the maintenance of a gold standard. In other words, the main object was to work at keeping up the gold value of the dollar, and not of the note; the gold value of the note, it was assumed, would naturally follow that of the dollar, and the gold reserve belonging to the former was only to be used for the purchase of silver to be coined into Straits dollars, the profit made therefrom being reconverted into gold for the purpose of maintaining exchange.

The conditions, however, in the Straits Settlements were the reverse of what they were in India. In India the rupee was the popular form of currency, and the notes formed a minor part of the currency system of the country; in the Straits Settlements the note was fast becoming the popular form of currency, and the dollars were being thrust out of circulation. There being no demand for dollars, no necessity arose for the coinage of extra dollars, as it did in India periodically for the coinage of extra rupees. There was, accordingly, no prospect of accumulating large reserves from the profits obtainable from a periodical coinage of dollars. It was evident, from the beginning that a gold standard reserve formed on such lines would be ridiculously inadequate for the purpose of maintaining the parity of exchange, and that it could not be effective without help from the gold assets of the Currency Note reserves. It is true that the gold standard fund was started on the profits obtained from the recoinage of the old Straits dollars into the smaller new Straits dollars. A sum of $4,751,800 was thus obtained, but it was small in comparison with the number of old Straits dollars in the Currency Reserve, which had come out of circulation owing to their displacement by currency notes. These, amounting to $12,960,000, were sold as bullion, and the gold was permitted to be held in London as part of the Note Guarantee Fund.

I now come to the reasons why the Indian method of procedure had to be departed from in the Straits Settlements. It was at first considered that dollars should only be given out in exchange for gold, but it was obvious, from the practice which sprung up in Singapore in modification of the procedure laid down by law, that it would not work. The procedure sanctioned by law was that coin should be given out in exchange for notes, but as the coin was immediately returned for notes of other denominations, the practice came into existence of

giving out notes of one denomination in exchange
for notes of other denominations without any inter-
change of coin. The books, of course, contain
entries of notes, being received in exchange for silver,
and the silver handed in again in exchange for notes
of other denominations. These are book entries
which cancel one another. Notes, therefore, came
to be given out direct in exchange for gold tendered
locally or to the Crown Agents in London, it being
obviously the most practicable and convenient
method. It was then suggested that the gold so
received should be handed over to a coinage department, which would supply the Currency Commissioners with its equivalent in Straits dollars, and
use the gold obtained from the profits on minting to
maintain the gold value of the dollar. There being,
however, no demand for dollars on the part of the
public, the proposal fell through. The conclusion
was forced on the Government that the best method
of maintaining exchange was to make use of the
machinery provided by the Currency Note Ordinance.
As will be seen further on, it eventually led to the
amalgamation of all the reserves.

The main operations necessary for maintaining
the parity of exchange are (*a*) the issue of local
currency at the fixed rate for gold tendered locally ;
(*b*) the withdrawal of local currency from circulation
and Bank reserves for gold issued locally at the fixed
rate ; (*c*) the issue of local currency at gold import
point for gold tendered in London ; (*d*) the withdrawal of local currency from circulation and Bank

reserves at gold export point for gold issued in London. These transactions having now been entrusted to the Currency Commissioners, and the note having gained in public favour the position of being the most acceptable form of currency in the Straits Settlements and Federated Malay States, the reserves held by the Currency Commissioners had naturally to be utilised for this purpose. All the large operations in connection with the issue and withdrawal of notes were operations for the adjustment of trade balances; and, though they incidentally served to confirm public belief in the facilities at the disposal of Government for the convertibility of their notes, the main purpose was the support of exchange. The gold standard reserve occupied a very minor place in these operations, and never came into play during the crisis of 1907-8, when our currency system was most severely tested.

The order in which these different funds would have been affected, in the event of a long and continued run on the Currency Commissioners' reserves, would have been somewhat as follows:—

1. Coin portion of the Note Guarantee Fund.

2. Investment portion of the Note Guarantee Fund.

3. Depreciation Fund.

4. Gold Standard Reserve,

and, lastly, the general revenue and surplus funds of the Colony in the event of the depletion of the above reserves.

G

During the crisis of 1907-8 it became clear that it was a positive disadvantage to hold separate funds earmarked for special objects, such as the gold standard reserve to deal with the deficiency in the bullion value of the metallic currency below its nominal value, and the depreciation fund to cover the depreciation in the market value of the securities below their cost price, and that it would be a distinct advantage to be able to use the readily realisable securities of one fund to meet the liabilities incurred on account of another without compelling the sale of its securities at a sacrifice or waiting for its depletion.

It was decided, therefore, to amalgamate all the funds and to hold one reserve against our currency notes, over-valued dollars, and subsidiary coin. All the profits of the note issue, viz., the income from investments and the profits from the sale and purchase of telegraphic transfers at gold points, as well as the profits from the coinage of dollars and subsidiary coins, were made payable into this fund. No payments were to be made to revenue until the accumulations of the fund completely covered all the Colony's liabilities in respect of its currency, viz., the difference between the bullion value and the token value of all the full legal tender silver coins, both in circulation and held in the reserve against notes, the difference between the bullion value and the token value of all the subsidiary coin, and the depreciation of the securities held in the investment portion of the Currency reserves.

*Legislation was introduced in 1913 to give effect to this decision, but the provision for rendering a separate account of the depreciation fund was retained, and the liability of revenue to make good separately the amounts due on account of depreciation remained, subject to the suspensory power vested in the Governor. It is not clear why the retention of this provision was insisted on. The bullion value of the silver in circulation and in the coin portion of the fund is as much liable to change as the market value of the securities in the investment portion, and the necessity for making special provision to make good the difference in the case of coin does not differ in any respect from the necessity for making good the difference in the case of securities. To my mind, it would have been more logical to have one account, so as to be able to ascertain at a glance the liability of revenue in respect of the whole legal tender currency of the Colony, power being reserved to the Governor to determine from time to time whether the whole or any portion of the liability should be paid into the the reserve out of revenue, or whether the payment should be altogether suspended.

An account kept in the following form would show clearly the liability of Government in respect of this currency :—

LIABILITIES.

Notes in circulation   x
Coin in circulation   ...   . a ———

*Given effect to finally by Ordinance V. of 1915. $x + a$

ASSETS.

Gold in Colony and London   ...   ...   *b*
Securities at market value   ...   ...   *c*
Silver coin in reserve at bullion value   *d*
Silver coin in circulation at bullion value   *e*
Government book debt $(x + a)—(b + c$
  $+ d + e)$ ...   .   ──────
                                            $x + a$

The question of satisfying the Government book
debt, whether in full or in part by payment out of
revenue, should be a matter for the Governor to
decide, subject to the sanction of the Secretary of
State, or, to be more constitutional, the payment
decided on by the Governor should be shown in the
Estimates as a service provided for by law, so as
not to interfere with the execution of the services
authorized in the Supply Ordinance.

A policy of extreme caution has been followed in
building up this reserve, so as to cover the difference
between the bullion value and the token value of
the subsidiary coinage.   So far as I know there is
no administration which keeps a reserve for
the purpose of redeeming subsidiary coin at its
face value, except the Government of Cyprus.   If
the subsidiary coin should fall below their token
value, the difficulty would be met by the Government withdrawing a portion of it and issuing full
legal tender coins in its place.   If only sufficient
subsidiary coin were minted, with a view to meeting
the needs of the people residing within the currency
area, and not with a view to making a large revenue

out of it in the expectation that the major part of it would be permanently absorbed elsewhere, there would be no difficulty in dealing with the problem. It does not seem to be right that this difference should be counted in to determine the amount of the book debt due from Government on account of their currency liabilities ; but, as under the most unfavourable circumstances, the redemption of a portion of the subsidiary coinage would fall on the dollar and the note, it seems only just that the profits from minting subsidiary coins should not, as in the past, be paid into revenue, but should be held in the currency reserve for the support of the gold par of exchange.

As regards India, the proposal to amalgamate the gold standard reserve with the Paper Currency Reserve, owing to the overlapping which so frequently occurred between the functions of the two reserves, was considered by the Royal Commission of 1913 on Indian Currency and Finance and rejected. They came to the conclusion that, under existing circumstances, the balance of advantage lay with the maintenance of separate reserves. The objections to an amalgamation are stated in Mr. L. Abraham's evidence as follows : " In view of the very sensitive and conservative Indian public opinion in these matters, to mix up a Paper Currency Reserve which serves one purpose, and a gold standard reserve which serves another purpose, might shake Indian public opinion ; the gold in the Paper Currency Reserve is meant to flow out in good times, and the assets of the gold standard reserve are meant to be kept intact for bad times, and the result of an amalgamation would be the dissipation of the gold in the Gold Standard Reserve in prosperous times."

In the words of the Report of the Royal Commission, the object of the Gold Standard Reserve is not to secure the convertibility on demand of the whole of the rupees in circulation, but only to provide a reserve, sufficient to convert into sterling such amount of rupees as may at any moment seek export in order to settle debts due in sterling. As regards the Paper Currency Reserve, the position of the Government is defined as follows: " The Government will not undertake to supply gold for internal purposes up to the full extent of the resources of the metallic portion of the Reserve, but when exchange reaches the gold export point, any gold in the Paper Currency Reserve in India should be given out only on such conditions as will secure its immediate export."

The enormous absorption of gold by India for hoarding and for conversion into ornaments, a form of investment which is popular amongst all classes of the native community, is a fact familiar to all. Whether the Government should help to encourage this unproductive habit, by giving gold freely out of the Paper Currency Reserve, is a matter which is open to doubt. But in the Straits Settlements and in the neighbouring States within the currency area there is no such large internal demand. It is true that, during the pilgrim season, a large demand for gold arises, but this gold is taken out of the country by the pilgrims and is not brought back. All the native demands for gold are for the purpose of export to India, Burmah, Siam, and China, and gold is known to have been exported to the Netherlands-Indies for the purpose of moving crops. The objections made to the amalgamation of these two reserves in India do not apply to the Straits Settlements, and no difficulty has been experienced in bringing about this reform.

Before proceding to the discussion of the question as to the amount of reserve necessary for securing the local convertibility of the note and the maintenance of exchange, it is necessary first to inquire into the nature of the holdings of the reserve, and to examine the developments which took place as regards its location.

As has already been seen, the reserve held against the note issue was divided into two :—

The coin portion consisting of silver dollars with a minimum limit of two-thirds of the circulation, afterwards reduced to one-half held entirely in Singapore ;

The investment portion with a maximum limit of one-third of the circulation, afterwards raised to one-half, the major part of which consisted of sterling securities (Consols, Colonial Government Stock, Corporation Stocks, &c.), held by the Crown Agents for the Colonies in London, and the balance consisting of Indian rupee paper held in the custody of the Comptroller and Accountant-General for India, for the Colonial Government.

These were the statutory limits, but in actual practice the coin portion held in Singapore was always kept somewhat in excess of the minimum limit of one-half.

With the initiation of the gold standard scheme, it became necessary to make provision for the receipt of gold by the Currency Commissioners in Singapore and the Crown Agents in London in exchange for notes. These measures were first introduced before the time came for fixing the dollar, so as to prevent any undue rise in the exchange value of the dollar, which, it was feared, would arise prematurely from the contraction of currency. There was no question, then, as to the location of the gold so received. It was provided that no gold should be kept, but that it should be used for the purchase of investments, and for the purchase of silver for coinage into dollars. The temporary rate, at which the exchange rate was to be fixed, was left to the Governor in Council, and was subject to the sanction of the Secretary of State. The Ordinances which gave effect to these measures were IV. of 1904 and III. of 1905. The latter ordinance made provision for carrying the profits on the minting of the dollars to a separate gold reserve, which was not to form part of the Note Guarantee Fund. Gold, apparently, was not to be held as part of the Note Guarantee Fund, except temporarily to enable investments to be bought, or silver to be purchased for conversion into dollars. Following the example of India, the gold reserve for the maintenance of exchange was to be built up on the profit from the coinage of dollars. These two Ordinances were never used, and were superseded by Ordinance I. of 1906, which came into force on the same day as the fixing of the dollar. Before the introduction of the 1906 Ordinance, the policy was adopted of receiving gold in Singapore only in exchange for notes issued there, owing to the difficulty as to the rate to be fixed for gold received in London, respecting which these two Ordinances of 1904 and 1905 were entirely silent. It was held at that time that the only sound course was to fix the rate for gold received in Singapore, as this plan was then considered sufficient to control exchange in both directions.

The difficulty was got over in Ordinance I. of 1906, by fixing the London rate at the gold import point based on the fixed rate of 2/4, and the cost of sending out gold to Singapore from London. Speedier relief could be given by obtaining the gold in London by cable than by waiting for its importation into Singapore; and the wild speculation which set in before the fixing of the dollar made the public believe that such speedy relief was a necessity. It was thought that the mere declaration of the rate would not be sufficient to ease the situation, but that an actual expansion of currency, which could only be obtained quickly by the tender of gold in London, was required. However, as it turned out, the Banks had a sufficiency of local currency in their vaults.

Although the Crown Agents were by this Ordinance enabled to receive gold in exchange for notes issued at Singapore, and it was made permissible to hold gold as part of the Note Guarantee Fund, instructions were given to the Crown Agents to despatch the gold received by them to Singapore.

Thus the policy of keeping the gold reserve in its entirety at Singapore was deliberately adopted and adhered to, until the force of circumstances became too strong and the policy had to be abandoned. What Lindsay foretold of the Government of India, that they must adopt his scheme despite themselves, proved also true of the Straits Government. The crisis of 1907-8 necessitated the sale of foreign remittances by Government, and, to do this, it became evident that the gold demanded should be kept where it was wanted, and where it could be given out to the purchasers with the least delay and at the least expense.

This crisis also demonstrated the fact that the old view that securities were the equivalent of cash and could readily be realised to meet any emergency, was untenable in the existing circumstances of the London money market. Even after this experience, it was held that there was no necessity to place gold on current account at the Bank of England, as the Crown Agents could always obtain gold in England, when necessary, on the security of investments, and that a gold reserve held in London would have no appreciably greater efficiency towards securing the immediate convertibility of the notes circulating in the Colony than have readily realisable securities held by the Crown Agents for the Colonies, the proceeds of which would, equally with gold held in London, be available to meet drafts issued in exchange for notes at Singapore.

During the period of this crisis, the gold at Singapore amounting to about £400,000, was rapidly drawn out for exportation. This was not sufficient to satisfy the external obligations of the Colony, and telegraphic transfers were sold by Government, which had to be met by the Crown Agents from the Colony's assets in their possession. Securities, which realised £504,566, were sold at a profit of £8,101; but it was admitted that no further securities could be sold without incurring considerable loss. Fortunately, a large loan had been raised by the Government, and the balance of the demand, amounting to nearly £500,000, was met out of the unexpended loan moneys, lying idle, on the security of the rest of the Currency Commissioners' investments.

These circumstances led to a review of the conditions under which the gold reserve of the Currency Commissioners was held. After consultation with the India Office, the recommendation was made that at any rate a substantial part of the gold reserve should be held in London. In confirming this recommendation, the Secretary of State wrote out to the Governor as follows : " To hold the reserve in London rather than in Singapore is to some extent a reversal of the policy previously advocated ; but I think it was recognised both by you and by my predecessor that the time might come when it would be more useful that the reserve should be in London, and recent events appear to me to show that this course will be in future more advantageous. The policy of holding gold in Singapore can hardly be said to have been a conspicuous success ; so far as I can see there is no object which would not equally be well attained by holding it in London ; and, of course, in the latter case, the gold would be earning interest, while it would be lying idle in Singapore."

On the introduction of the bill to give effect to this proposal, the Singapore Chamber of Commerce expressed themselves as strongly in favour of the gold being held in Singapore rather than in London. They considered that stability of exchange and confidence in the currency would be best established by the retention of the gold in Singapore, and that it was necessary, for the purpose of balancing international trade, that gold should be imported into the Colony. The unofficial members of the Council also took the same view, and opposed the provisions of the Bill intended to effect this purpose.

It will be remembered that there was an agitation in India, which had the same object in view, and which was one of the causes that led to the appointment, in 1913, of the Royal Commission on Indian Currency and Finance. The following is the view of the Commission on this subject :—

" The most suitable place for the location of the

Gold Standard Reserve is, in our opinion, undoubtedly London, and in this view the majority of our witnesses concurred. London is the clearing house of the world, India's chief customer is the United Kingdom, and London is the place where the money is required both for the expenditure of the Secretary of State on behalf of India, and for payment of India's commercial obligations to this country and the world in general. If the reserve were kept in India it would have to be shipped to London to be used. This would involve delay at a moment when immediate action is essential. The objections put forward to keeping it in London rest on the belief that the reserve is regarded in London as being available to supplement the Bank of England's reserve. There is no foundation at all for this belief. We have no hesitation, therefore, in recommending that the whole of the Gold Standard Reserve be kept in London."

Ordinance XXVII. of 1908, which was brought in to enable the Currency Commissioners to hold a part of their reserve in gold in London, provided that the proportion of gold to silver should as soon as practicable be raised to two of gold to one of silver. This gave a silver reserve of one-sixth and a gold reserve of one-third of the notes in circulation, the investment reserve being left untouched. This provision was not agreed to by the home authorities, and the proportion authorized was a minimum limit of one-third of the note circulation to be held entirely in legal tender silver in the

Colony, and a limit of one-sixth of the note circulation to be held in gold by the Crown Agents for the Colonies in London. The limit of one-half of the note circulation for the investment portion of the fund being a maximum limit, the Crown Agents could hold gold temporarily at the expense of this portion of the fund.

Though no legislative sanction was given to these instructions of the Secretary of State's, pending the introduction of fresh legislation to cover all the currency operations of the Government, these instructions were followed as far as possible. The silver in the Currency Commissioners' Reserve remained far in excess of the one-third limit, and there was no immediate means of reducing it except by selling part of it as bullion for gold. The arrangements made to divert to London shipments of gold intended for Singapore, did not apply to such countries as India, China, Japan, or the Netherlands-Indies, and a certain amount of gold always continued to come in. Like the sale of the new reduced dollar as bullion, the shipment of such gold to London at the cost of Government is too expensive an operation to embark upon if it could be avoided, so that the coin portion of the fund located in the Colony will always hold a certain proportion of gold. With the great expansion of the note issue caused by the tender of gold, the silver portion of the coin reserve held at Singapore had fallen well below the one-third limit, then fixed as a minimum, which the Currency Commissioners were bound to hold in the Colony in silver legal tender coin.

The question as to the amount of the silver reserve to be held at Singapore was again raised in 1910. The case made out for a reduction cannot be better put than in the Governor's words :—

" The main objection to keeping so large a proportion of silver dollars in our reserve is that for the main purpose of a reserve in the case of a currency like that of the Colony, it is useless.

" The object of having a reserve, in our case, is to be in a position to contract the circulation, when, in time of depression, it becomes redundant and exchange goes heavily against us. As the dollar has ceased to be an international coin, and has become a promise to pay like the note, we cannot contract our currency by giving dollars for notes, and the larger the proportion of dollars we maintain, the weaker our reserve becomes, and the more liable we are to have to sell securities at a time when others are doing the same and the price is low.'

" A reserve of silver dollars, while the dollar is so much overvalued as to be practically a promise to pay, is useless in case of a panic due to causes affecting the credit of the Government. It might be of some use in case, say, there was a large issue of forged notes in circulation, but it is improbable that such an occurrence would affect notes of more then one denomination, and, if so, it would probably take the form of a demand for notes of other denominations than of a demand for silver coin, which is more liable to be counterfeited than notes. The only practical use, therefore, of a silver reserve is to be in a position to meet an expansion of the silver circulation without having recourse to further minting. For that purpose a reserve of one-fifth is ample."

This was written in July, 1910. In 1912 there were forgeries of five dollar notes on a considerable scale. The correctness of Sir John Anderson's anticipation is demonstrated by the fact that the forgeries affected only the currency of the five-dollar notes, and the form the demand took was not for silver dollars, but for one-dollar and ten-dollar notes.

A minimum silver reserve of one-fifth of the note circulation was eventually agreed to, on the condition that the coin reserve in the Colony should not be allowed to fall below one-third of the notes in circulation, the balance to be held in sovereigns. The proportions finally authorized, and given effect to by legislation in 1913, were as follows :—

I. A minimum coin reserve of one-half of the note circulation.

II. A maximum investment reserve of one-half of the note circulation.

The coin reserve (I.) was apportioned as follows :—

(*a*) A minimum coin reserve of one-third of the note circulation to be held in the Colony, consisting of

(*b*) A minimum silver reserve of one-fifth of the

note circulation; and (*c*) the balance—a maximum of two-fifteenths of the notes in circulation—to be held in gold in the Colony.

(*d*) A maximum gold reserve of one-sixth of the note circulation to be held in London by the Crown Agents for the Colonies.

The amalgamation of the Depreciation Fund and the Gold Standard Reserve with the Note Guarantee Fund will, of course, increase the dimensions of the portions of the funds as fixed by Statute. The depreciation fund, being all in investments, could increase II. beyond its statutory limit, and the gold standard reserve being kept in London, partly in gold and partly in investments, would increase I. (*d*) and II. beyond their statutory limits. I. (*d*) could also be increased at the expense of II.

These regulations seem to me cumbrous and inelastic and likely to interfere with the free, automatic working of the currency scheme. For instance, the fixing of a minimum coin reserve of one-third of the circulation to be held in the Colony, of which one-fifth of the circulation must be kept as a minimum silver holding, means that the gap must be kept filled either by the importation of gold from the London Reserve at some expense to Government, or by refusing to give out gold freely in the Colony in exchange for notes. My firm belief is that it will be found impossible to work the scheme, on the conditions laid down, without causing much harm to trade and much expense to Government. Gold should be allowed to come in freely and

H

spontaneously where it is required, and where it demands admittance. In my opinion, the best solution would be to have no rigid restrictions as to limits and localities; but that subject, say, to a minimum silver holding in the Colony of one-fifth of the total currency reserve, every facility should be given for the free movement of gold as trade requires it.

This does not imply that the balance of the reserve should be held in gold in a liquid form, viz., in actual cash or in bankers' money. It has been found practicable to invest a considerable portion of it in permanent securities without in any way interfering with the movement of money for the purposes of trade; but the question is, is it safe or profitable to hold such a large proportion as one-half of the reserve in permanent securities?

The enormous depreciation in value of what were considered to be the cream of first-class securities has been a striking feature of recent years. Most of the great London Banks have been compelled to write off very large sums on account of depreciation of gilt-edged securities, especially of Consols. The failure of the Birkbeck Bank was mainly due to their inability to realize the cost price of their investments, which were all in first-class securities. The position of some of the industrial banks, such as the Yorkshire Penny Bank, was in great danger owing to the same cause.

The total depreciation from year to year in the value of the Currency Commissioners' investments is shown in the following table for a period of ten years :—

Year.	Cost Price of Securities.	Market Value.	Depreciation.
	Dollars.	Dollars.	Dollars.
1904	6,455,477	5,561,044	894,433
1905	7,531,206	5,897,336	1,633,870
1906	7,610,707	5,616,089	1,994,618
1907	11,673,679	9,407,434	2,266,245
1908	9,405,064	7,336,409	2,069,655
1909	9,106,852	6,975,645	2,131,207
1910	13,879,394	11,571,550	2,307,844
1911	16,319,381	13,915,342	2,404,039
1912	21,165,749	18,318,028	2,847,721
1913	22,162,935	18,664,940	3,497,995

Since 1907-8 there has been a further and even more marked depreciation in the value of Consols and other Government Stock. The conclusion arrived at by the Royal Commission on Indian Currency and Finance, is that even the finest securities can no longer be regarded as identical with cash in the sense in which they were so regarded fifteen or twenty years ago, and their realization might involve such a loss in capital value and such an aggravation of a crisis, which it would be India's direct interest to allay, as to making the holding of more than a comparatively moderate proportion of such stock undesirable in the case of the Gold Standard Reserve.

In the Annual Report of the Java Bank for the year 1911-12, it is stated that the Bank has made it a point to avoid Government Stock as an investment for its capital and reserve fund, unless the securities fell due within a short time and were redeemable at least at their price of issue, and the Bank has, therefore, been able to avoid the losses which the heavy decline in the value of Government securities would otherwise have caused.

The maximum limit of one-half for the investment portion of the fund is, I think, much too large. The original limit of one-third is sufficiently large to ensure a good working income, especially as permission has now been given to hold half of the gold portion of the coin reserve, in the custody of the Crown Agents, in Treasury bills and other short-dated loans and cash at call.

The reasons given as to the necessity for holding the other half in actual specie form a reversal of the previous instructions, that it was not necessary to keep gold on current account with the Bank of England. To meet remittances by realizing securities, or by borrowing against the securities in the investment portion of the fund, would mean that the gold would be provided at the expense of the general gold reserve of the United Kingdom, which was, in the opinion of many persons amongst those who were most competent to judge, already far from adequate to the commercial needs of the country; and though the transactions of the Straits Settlements Government would not, for the present at any rate, be sufficiently considerable to exercise any appreciable influence on the general gold reserve of the United Kingdom, in view of the existing state of commercial feeling on the subject, recognition should be given to the principle that a Colonial Goverment adopting for its own convenience an arrangement, which depends for its effective working on the free market for gold existing in London, ought to do something, at any rate, towards maintaining the actual reserve of specie on which that free market depends.

The questions still left for examination in this chapter are the nature of the holdings in the currency reserve, and the amount adequate for the purpose of securing the convertibility of the note and of maintaining the parity of exchange.

The provision by law as to the nature of the investment portion of the Note Guarantee Fund was as follows:—It was allowed to be invested in Indian Government securities and such securities of the Government of the United Kingdom or of the Government of any British Colony, other than the Straits Settlements, as may from time to time be approved of by a Secretary of State; not more than one-half, however, of such sum was to be invested in Indian Government securities, except by the express sanction of the Secretary of State.

The major part of the investments consist of Colonial Government securities and Consols. The Crown Agents for the Colonies are, therefore, able to finance other Colonies in the matter of loans, and to employ the fruits of the economic system of currency possessed by the Straits Settlements to the advantage of every Colony, except that of the Colony possessing the currency.

In 1907, when the first Straits Settlements' loan was raised, it was suggested by the Crown Agents that the Currency Note Ordinance might well be amended so as to allow the investment of a portion of the Note Guarantee Fund in the securities of the Colony. The Government were in favour of the suggestion, and proposed that provision should be made so as to enable a portion of the fund, not exceeding one-quarter, to be invested in the securities of the Straits Settlements Government. The proposal was not approved. " If investments were to be made in Straits Settlements' Stock," wrote the Secretary of State, " it would be just as well (so far as security is concerned) to spend the sum in question without investing it at all, since Straits Settlements' Stock is only secured by the general revenue of the Colony on which the notes are already a prior charge."

When the proposal was eventually approved by the Secretary of State, and legislation was introduced to consolidate the Currency Notes Ordinance with amendments, this particular provision was opposed by the unofficial members of Council, on the ground that it provided the same guarantee as that on which the notes were ultimately secured, and that the investment part of the Currency Reserve should be secured by the independent guarantee of other administrations having no connection with the Colony.

If the principle that the whole of a token currency must be covered in full either in cash, or in cash and securities readily convertible into cash, is right, then the justification for holding the Colony's securities in the Guarantee Fund is that the securities are marketable and are more readily realisable than most of the other stock held by the Currency Commissioners. The holding of this stock by the Currency Commisioners does not throw any additional liability on the revenue of the Colony than if they were held by private persons, and the position of a private holder of Straits Settlements' Stock is a good deal sounder than that of a holder in some of the Colonial Government Securities which form part of the investment portion of the Guarantee Fund.

But there is a much broader view taken of this question, a view the Indian authorities had no hesitation in adopting from the very beginning of the institution of their paper currency, and which is founded on the well-known doctrines of Ricardo and John Stuart Mill.

"A currency is in its most perfect state," says

Ricardo, " when it consists of paper money, but of paper money of an equal value with the gold which it professes to represent. The use of paper instead of gold substitutes the cheapest in place of the most expensive medium, and enables the country, without loss to any individual, to exchange all the gold, which it before used for this purpose, for raw materials, utensils and food, by the use of which both its wealth and its enjoyments are increased." As he writes elsewhere, it releases a commodity which becomes productive in the form of other commodities, instead of remaining unproductive in the form of coin.*

It is not necessary, he says, that paper money should be payable in specie to secure its value; it is only necessary that the quantity should be regulated according to the value of the metal which is declared to be the standard. Just as metallic currency is observed to increase with every fall in the value of the metal which forms the standard, so paper might be increased with every fall in the value of gold, if gold were the standard. Whenever the price of bullion rose above Mint price, further issues of paper currency would cease, or, if necessary, the existing issues would be contracted by the delivery of uncoined bullion at the Mint price, in exchange for notes, until the price of bullion and the Mint price were again in accordance. To a superficial observer, the reverse of this process

* Ricardo's "Principles of Political Economy and Taxation," Chapter xxvii,

appears to go on in the Straits, but this is not so. In the Straits every fall in the value of gold, the exchange standard, means a rise in the exchange value of the dollar, a rise in gold prices and a fall in silver prices, and the currency then is in need of expansion. Similarly, when there is a rise in the price of gold, there is a fall in the exchange value of the dollar, gold prices fall and silver prices rise, and the currency is then in need of contraction to gravitate to the fixed value.

Mill, in his examination of this theory, whilst admitting that such a currency would not be subject to any of the evils inherent in an inconvertible paper currency, did not consider that it would secure the confidence of the public, being of opinion that the most important consideration was to gain and retain that confidence by adhering to a simple principle intelligent to the most untaught capacity. He adds that the only advantage of the system was the exemption from the necessity of keeping any reserve of the precious metals; which is not a very important consideration, especially as a Government, so long as its good faith is not suspected, need not keep so large a reserve as private issuers, being not so liable to great and sudden demands, since there never can be any real doubt of its solvency.

Whilst, therefore, deciding in favour of a convertible currency, payable in specie, he is in agreement with Ricardo that the value saved to the community by dispensing with a metallic currency should be a clear gain to those who provide the substitute. If the substitute is issued by Government and employed in paying off debt, it would probably become productive capital; if used for Government services, it would relieve taxation, in which case the amount is saved by the taxpayers at large, who either add it to their capital or spend it as income. The result is summed up as follows :—

" *The substitution, therefore, of paper for the precious metals, should always be carried as far as is consistent with safety ; no greater amount of metallic currency being retained than is necessary to maintain, both in fact and in public belief, the convertibility of the paper.*"*

Until 1905, the whole of the investment portion of the Paper Currency Reserve in India consisted of Indian Rupee paper. When the limit for securities was extended from ten to fourteen crores of rupees, four crores were allowed to be invested in sterling securities as a maximum holding, one of the reasons being that it was inadvisable to hold too large holdings of a security which was likely to be depreciated by the same causes as would possibly entail a run on the Paper Currency reserve. It will thus be seen that the Indian Government made use of their currency reserve in supporting their internal loans and in thus helping the development of their country.

The Royal Commission of 1913 propose to go still further, and to increase the amount available for investment to one-third of the net or actual

* J. S. Mill. "Principles of Political Economy." Book III, Chap. XXII.

circulation, plus the amount of the notes held in
the Reserve Treasuries, which carries the amount
available for investment to 47 per cent. of the gross
circulation on the figures as they then stood. They
further recommend that power should be given to
make temporary loans to the Banks so as to ease
the stringency of currency during the busy season,
so long as the cash portion of the fund does not fall
below two-thirds of the net or actual circulation.

It is seen, then, that the Indian Government
recognise the principle that the profits yielded them
by their economy of the precious metals should be
used to finance their loans and to help their money
market in times of stringency. There is this further
and important difference between the Indian system
and the Straits Settlements system. In the former,
the whole of the income from investments is paid
into general revenue, in the latter it is paid into a
depreciation fund until the whole of the cost price
of the securities is fully paid.

The same principle governed the action of the
Indian authorities in applying a portion of the Gold
Standard Reserve to capital expenditure on Railways.
There is no essential difference in principle between
the Gold Standard Reserve and the Paper Currency
Reserve. The one guarantees the gold value of the
rupee in circulation, or rather of that portion of
it which seeks export for the adjustment of trade
balances; the other guarantees the rupee value of
the notes in circulation and to a certain extent their
gold value. The main difference between the two

is that, while the paper currency has no intrinsic value, the silver contained in the over-valued rupee is an asset of considerable value.

Sir David Barbour, who was a member of the Committee which made the suggestion to employ a part of the Gold Standard Reserve fund on railways, gives the following explanation in his book, "The Standard of Value."

" It makes practically no difference, whether you reduce your borrowing by using a portion of the gold reserve for capital expenditure on railways, or maintain your borrowing at its full amount, and invest the whole of the gold reserve in gold securities. In the former case, you can borrow in case of need up to the amount which has been used to reduce borrowing, and still be in quite as good a position as if the whole of the gold reserve had been invested. The reduction of the amount borrowed in London strengthened the Indian exchange."

The Royal Commission did not condemn this action, though they considered that no diversion similar to that made in 1907 for railway development should, under any circumstances, be permitted until further experience allowed of a much more accurate definition of the calls which the Reserve may have to meet than is at present possible.

Before passing on to the question of the adequacy of the reserve to be held against our note and over-valued silver currency, it would be well to mention one other form of holding which forms such a prominent feature of all Continental note issues, although in view of the constitution of the Currency Commissioners, it can hardly be regarded as practicable in the Straits Settlements.

The question has been frequently put to me why notes are not issued to discount bills, and it is submitted that the foreign credits held by Banks possessing note issues are the first line of defence for meeting an adverse balance of trade, as in the form they are held, they are quite as liquid as gold, and in addition the expense of transporting gold for the purpose of adjusting foreign obligations is thereby avoided; that the need for a temporary expansion of currency can be best and most automatically met in this way without the expense of increasing the metallic reserves.

The general experience is that the security of first-class bills is excellent, and that the risk of loss is infinitesimal, especially if the business be confined to a rediscount of good bills for the Banks. The result of this system in Java has been that the replenishing of its gold reserve in Europe is no longer dependent on the exhaustion of the currency reserves of the local banks, as it is in the Straits Settlements, and the currency keeps in touch with the expansion of trade within the country and with every stage of its development without any unnecessary movement of the precious metals.

Indian official opinion is not against such an extension of the functions of the Note issue. The evidence given by Mr. Lionel Abrahams, of the

India office, on this point before the Royal Commission is interesting and instructive. It is as follows :—

"If you will not unduly shock commercial opinion in India, I think it would be an enormous improvement if arrangements were made by which additional notes would be issued at suitable times, especially in the busy season, either uncovered altogether or, what I should prefer, because it would look better, against security that can suitably be held for a short time. Supposing there were first-class bills which became due to be paid off three or four months after the date on which they were received, then by putting such securities in the Paper Currency Reserve and issuing notes against them, there would be a possibility of elasticity without any risk worth considering, in fact, without any risk at all, and I think trade and other interests would benefit by it."

Although there is no prospect in the near future of introducing this arrangement in the Straits' currency system, there is room for much needed extensions of the Currency Reserves. Provided that an adequate reserve in cash and money at short notice were always maintained, the Currency Reserve might, with great advantage to the State, be used in making loans on good security and at reasonable interest to such public bodies as the Harbour Board, the several Municipalities, and the Federated Malay States Railway Administration, if not unreservedly, at any rate at times when it is inconvenient and expensive to raise loans, and when the urgency of the public works of these bodies requires the immediate issue of money. The money in the Currency Reserve would then become productive capital within the country in which the currency is used, and would fulfil the main purpose of an economic currency—the general gain and advantage of the States and the community.

The effects of the financial crisis of 1907-8, which were felt severely in all the Eastern countries, excepting Java, were accentuated in the Straits Settlements by the demonetization of the Straits dollar in Sumatra and the Siamese Malay States, in which countries our dollars were current to the exclusion of the Netherlands guilder and the Siamese tical. The payment of the award for the expropriation of the Tanjong Pagar Docks by Government, a large part of which was demanded locally, also helped to increase the strain. The crisis was, thus, more prolonged in the Straits Settlements than in the other countries affected.

The strain on the gold assets of the Currency Commissioners will be seen from the following table, which gives their sterling assets as they stood on the 30th September, 1907, immediately before the effects of the financial crisis of 1907-8 were first felt in the Colony, and as they stood on the 31st January, 1909, when these assets were at their lowest point.

	30th September, 1907.	31st January, 1909.
	Dollars.	Dollars.
Gold held at Singapore at £7 to 60 dols.	4,383,460	40,620
Gold held in London ...		
Value of Securities (including depreciation fund), cost price at £7 to 60 dols.	10 438,560	6,279,300
Remittance to Crown Agents for investment...	3,276,935	——
	18,103,955	6,319,928

The gold assets were thus reduced by a dollar value of $11,784,027, or a reduction of 65 per cent.

The silver reserve in the Currency vaults increased from $10,157,279 on 30th September, 1907, to $21,148,227, an increase of $10,990,948. The note circulation at these dates was $27,362,555 and $26,065,505 respectively, so that the gross circulation, including reserves in banks and Government treasuries, and excluding subsidiary coin, was $52,105,852 and $39,817,844, or a decrease of $12,288,008, or very nearly a reduction of 22 per cent. Fully 10 per cent. of this was probably due to the demonetization in Sumatra and Siam.

It will be observed that the reduction was not effected by any considerable withdrawal of notes, which, being the form of currency in demand, remained in circulation, but by a very large withdrawal of dollars, for which there was no public demand, from circulation.

Under the currency scheme, when gold is required for the purpose of adjusting international trade balances, it cannot be drawn out without causing a corresponding reduction in the currency in circulation. The purpose of recent legislation is to cover fully every note, dollar, and subsidiary coin in circulation. It is inconceivable that such a state of things would ever occur as would cause the presentation of every note, dollar, or subsidiary coin for redemption. There is the irreducible minimum, the minimum of currency required to finance the daily wants of the community, and which must always remain in circulation. Experience also shows us that, when gold is drawn out in such amounts as to make the contraction of currency so severe as to hamper transactions within the country, gold will naturally flow in again and release local currency to relieve the situation.

All that the Government should be prepared to do is to arrange for the redemption of a certain proportion of the currency in circulation and to place themselves in a position of absolute safety.

In determining what that proportion should be, the practice in other countries of dealing with their currency reserves will form a useful guide.

I will first take the proposals made in the Annexe to the Report of the Royal Commission of 1913 for the regulation of the reserves against the Indian Note issue. The following account is there given.

	Crores.		Crores.
Gross circulation of notes	65	Government book debt...	10
		Consols	10
		Approved securities and bills of exchange pledged	6
		Gold	15
		Rupees	24
	65		65

The coin portion amounts to 60 per cent., the rupees coming to 37 per cent., and the gold to 23 per cent.; securities amount to a little more than 15 per cent., loans on securities and bills of exchange to .92 per cent.; and the Government book debt, for funds placed at the disposal of Government without special cover or interest, to a little more than 15 per cent. This item is a substitution for the Indian Government paper held in the fund and is to bear no interest.

It will be seen that only 85 per cent. of the note issue will be covered by coin, consols, approved securities, and bills of exchange. It is further proposed that by paying a tax on the excess, the fiduciary issue be increased from 40 per cent. to 60 per cent. so that the cover in coin will be reduced from 60 per cent. to 40 per cent. of the note issue, on this condition, however, that the proportion of cash shall never be allowed to fall below 40 per cent. of the notes in circulation. This is stated to be the equivalent of what the German Reichsbank keeps,

With the omission of a taxable excess of the fiduciary issue, the practice in Java, where the conditions most nearly resemble those of the Straits Settlements, is very similar to this.

The issue of notes there has been granted by charter to the Java Bank. There is no limit to the issue, no prescribed minimum, any excess over which is subject to taxation as is the case with most Continental State banks, and as is now recommended for India in the Annexe to the Report of the Royal Commission.

The Java Bank is obliged to keep against their notes in circulation, their unpaid short term drafts and credit balances, a reserve of at least 40 per cent. in bullion, of which at least 75 per cent., or 30 per cent. of their liabilities, must be kept in Netherlands-India, 15 per cent. being kept in Netherlands-India in legal tender currency.

From their report for 1912, the last I have access to, their metallic reserve amounted to 50 per cent. of their note issue and 46 per cent. of their total liabilities, their invested capital and reserve funds, foreign bills and short loans in Holland, to 30 per cent. of their note issue, or 26 per cent. of their total liabilities; so that for their note issue they had a cover of 87 per cent., or, leaving out their invested capital and reserve funds, a cover of 80 per cent. for their note issue and of 73 per cent. for their total liabilties in readily realizable assets. There is no reserve against thetr token guilders and subsidiary coin.

In Japan, the proportion of bullion reserve to note issue was, in 1911, 57.56 per cent.; in 1912, 55·81 per cent.; in 1913, 56.98 per cent. The management of the note issue is in the hands of the Bank of Japan, and this reserve serves as cover for the other liabilities of the Bank as well. So far as I can gather from the information available to me, their coin reserve is well under 40 per cent. of their total liabilities. They hold no reserve against their silver coins in circulation which are not taken into account in their total liabilities.

In Canada, the notes in circulation up to a limit of thirty million dollars are covered only to the extent of 25 per cent. in gold and guaranteed securities, the gold forming not less than 15 per cent. of the circulation. Above thirty millions, the notes must be fully covered by bullion or specie.

The position of the Bank of France on the 31st December, 1913, and 2nd April, 1914, is shown in the subjoined returns :—

31st *December*, 1914.

Notes in circulation £228,542,040	Gold £140,695,650
	Silver... ... 25,602,520
Accounts current ... 39,147,420	
£267,689,460	£166,298,170

2nd *April*, 1914.

Notes in circulation £238,915,520	Gold £144,625,360
	Silver... ... 25,072,280
Accounts current ... 31,091,200	
£270,006,720	£169,697,640

This gives a reserve of practically 60 per cent. of the total liabilities of the Bank. This appears to be the proportion normally maintained between the liabilities and the bullion assets of the Bank.

The Times newspaper, of the 26th November, 1914, gives the following for the Bank of England. Owing to the abnormal times we are passing through, they cannot be regarded as typical of their ordinary holdings, but they are instructive as giving some indication of the proportion of bullion to paper currency considered necessary. The gold reserve of the Bank had by that date increased by twenty-five millions since the beginning of the war.

The Bank of England returns show a holding of coin and bullion of £71,618,945, securities amounting to £7,434,900, and a Government debt of £11,015,100, against a note circulation of £90,063,945. The note circulation in England, however, occupies a very minor place as compared with the system of cheques, and the earmarking of such a large coin reserve for the sole purpose of securing the notes is, in the opinion of many competent judges, the reason why the note system is restricted and inelastic, and that cheques have been found to be an effective substitute for them.*

*The British Bank Act of 1844, on which the Indian Paper Currency and the Straits Note Issue were modelled, is held by many competent judges to be responsible for the want of economy and elasticity manifested in the working of the note system established in England, and the prediction that it would fail to work satisfactorily in times of commercial crisis of an aggravated type has been proved to be true by the suspension of the Act on more than one such occasion. By this Act, the fiduciary portion of the note issues, that is, the portion issued on securities, was never to exceed a certain limit, which was

It will be seen from the foregoing that although the legal minimum coin reserve has in some cases been fixed at 40 per cent. of the note circulation, yet in actual practice the coin holding has been maintained at between 50 and 60 per cent. of the note circulation.   It should, however, be borne in mind that on the Continent, and in Java and Japan,

fixed as low as possible, and all the other issues, to which no limit was fixed, had to be in exchange for coin or bullion.   The increase of currency and extension of credit required in times of trade activity were, accordingly, provided by means of bank deposits and the consequent development of the cheque system, owing to the difficulty of procuring notes without the actual tender of bullion or coin.   Another drawback was the high limit of the lowest denomination of note.   It is stated that the chief reason for the establishment of such a high minimum in 1826, was that, owing to the frequent failure of banks of issue prior to that year, it was considered desirable that protection should be afforded to the poorer classes against losses from such causes.   Five-pound notes are not a very convenient form of currency, much too high for the use of ordinary purchasers.   It is said that the run on the Bank of England during the closing days of July, 1914, was due mainly to this cause, the necessity for smaller change which could not conveniently be obtained elsewhere, and not to any large extent to a feeling of nervousness on the part of the public.   The suspension of the Bank Act, which would only have enabled the Bank to make a further issue of notes, not under five pounds, unsecured by gold, would not have relieved the situation, as gold would still have been required for smaller payments.   The issue of Treasury notes of £1 and 10s. with an unlimited legal tender, which were issued to the Banks when required to the extent of 20 per cent. of their deposits, relieved the situation and restored public confidence.   It will be remembered that the issue of $1 notes as unlimited legal tender in the Straits Settlements in 1906, when the silver reserve of the Currency Commissioners was sent abroad for recoinage, had a like effect.

no distinction is made between the reserve held against the note issue and the reserve held against other banking liabilities.

It has been seen that during the crisis of 1907-8 a contraction of only 22 per cent. of the gross circulation of notes and dollars took place. Not less than 10 per cent., probably about 12 per cent., of this is due to the expansion of currency caused by the demonetization of the Straits dollars in Sumatra and Siam and the payment of the Tanjong Pagar award.

*Having regard to all considerations, I think that a cover of 85 per cent. will be ample under the worst conditions possible; and, in view of the public preference for notes, that a silver reserve of 20 per cent. is a sufficient holding to be maintained in the Colony. There is not much objection to making it a minimum holding. To make it a hard and fast rule, however, as to a minimum coin holding of gold and silver in the Colony seems to me to be a mistaken policy, for it will interfere with the free movement of gold, as the gap between the minimum silver holding and the minimum coin reserve in the Colony must be kept filled by refusing

---

*A greater portion of the Currency Reserves could, in fact, be released, with absolute safety, for employment for local purposes than is allowable by public belief. It is for this reason that I have consistently advocated that our currency should be secured on the revenues of the Federated Malay States as well on those of the Colony. Public belief in the soundness of our currency will then be so strengthened as to enable the Government to retain no larger amount of metallic currency than is consistent with safety.

to give gold when it is demanded, whenever a shrinkage of the local coin reserve to the minimum limit occurs.

The proportions I am in favour of are :—

A minimum silver holding of unlimited legal tender in the Colony of 20 per cent. of the gross circulation of notes and dollars.

Forty per cent. in gold of the gross circulation to be held in the Colony and in London, not according to fixed proportions, but in accordance with the requirements of trade; half of the portion located in London being held in the form of cash at call or money at short notice ; and the balance of 25 per cent. to be held in permanent securities at their market value, including Straits Settlements Stock to an amount not exceeding 10 per cent.

The accumulations of the fund, beyond the 85 per cent., might safely be used by Government for the repayment of debt and capital expenditure, preferably on productive undertakings. The Commissioners of Currency should also have the power to lend such moneys at moderate rates of interest to such public bodies as the Harbour Boards, Municipalities, Railway Administration, etc., on the security of a charge on their revenues, or what comes to the same thing, invest such accumulations in the public loans of these bodies, especially if such loans are insufficiently supported by the public. In the event of any undue stringency of money in the market, advances could also be made to the Banks, on the deposit of approved securities, which should include Municipal debentures and local stock that might hereafter be raised by the Governments of the Straits Settlements, or of the Federated Malay Straits, or by the Harbour Boards. By the extension ot the issues of local stock, native capital will gradually find another outlet besides the investment in town building land which has had the effect of enhancing the price of land and of raising rents—a matter which presses so cruelly on the poorer classes of the community.

A great and much needed help will thus be given, with no risk at all, to the internal development of the countries and to the growth of the welfare of the communities within the area of circulation of the currency of the Straits Settlements.

CHAPTER VI

Remittances

REMITTANCES are of the following descriptions :—

Remittances by the Government to the Crown Agents for the Colonies in London for their current requirements, for the payments due in the United Kingdom for such services as pensions, leave salaries, interest on loans, and for the purchase of materials for public works. These are always made through the Exchange Banks by telegraphic transfers, and the Crown Agents' account is so fed, when exchange is favourable, as to enable them to have sufficient funds in hand for two or three months' requirements. There has not been so much difference in recent years between the rates of interest obtainable in London and Singapore from the Banks, so that the balance of advantage lies with this system, as unfavourable rates of exchange are avoided when remittances are not made monthly for each month's requirements without regard to the rates obtainable. More favourable rates are also generally obtainable in Singapore than in London.

As regards the Federated Malay States, the Crown Agents have, up to very recently, drawn on Kuala

Lumpor every month through the Exchange Banks ; but this has now, I believe, been altered, and the Straits practice has been adopted. When exchange at any time reaches the gold import point then obtaining, these remittances will go through the Currency Commissioners.

Remittances by Crown Agents to Singapore.

These are very few in number, and only take place in exceptional circumstances, if loan moneys in the hands of the Crown Agents should ever be required in the Colony. These are made through the Exchange Banks at the current rate, but, should exchange be at the gold export point when such a remittance is due, they would be made through the Currency Commissioners.

Remittances to India for settlement, chiefly of Money Order transactions, which always show a heavy adverse balance against the Straits and Federated Malay States. These are paid by gold drafts on London in favour of the Bombay Post Office, or by cheques on a joint account kept by the Colony and Federated Malay States with the Chartered Bank of India, Australia, and China at Calcutta. This account is fed when Indian exchange is favourable to the Colony, and the remittances in this case are made, and will always be made, through the Exchange Banks. The gold drafts in favour of Bombay would, like the remittances to the Crown Agents, go through the Currency Commissioners when exchange reaches the specie import point.

The other Government remittances are very small,

and are hardly worth mentioning. Ceylon and Hong Kong are settled direct by drafts through the Exchange Banks, and, as regards the other Colonies, accounts are usually adjusted through the Crown Agents.

These remittances present no difficulties ; but it is not so with the remittances on account of the Currency Commissioners. There are two distinct operations in connection with their remittances. There is the movement originating with the Commissioners for the adjustment of the reserves held in London—the investment portion and the gold portion—so as to accord with the proportion fixed by Statute. Secondly, there is the movement originating with the public for the adjustment of trade balances, for the sale or purchase of transfers on London, according as the balance is favourable or unfavourable to the Colony.

These two distinct operations have been rather mixed up, and we stand in this curious and anomalous position. Though there is no statutory provision to the effect, it has been the practice for the Currency Commissioners to make remittances through the Banks, when exchange was favourable, for the purchase of securities for the investment portion of the Currency Guarantee Fund. This has not been objected to either by the Secretary of State for the Colonies or the Lord Commissioners of the Treasury, and there has been no local opposition to this practice. It may here be remarked that, as the law stands at present, the investment portion of the fund may extend to one-half the amount of the notes in circulation. As regards the gold portion in London which can only extend to one-sixth of the notes in circulation, recent instructions put the Currency Commissioners in this curious position. They can only transport gold from Singapore, or divert to London intended shipments of gold to Singapore from Australia and Egypt, or purchase remittances from the Banks at the gold import point. All these operations are expensive and wasteful. The Currency Commissioners can remit through the Banks, if they want gold to purchase securities; but if they want to keep the same gold in a liquid state so as to meet their liabilities with readiness and ease, they cannot do so, but are compelled to wait until the trade balance pushes exchange up to the import point, or makes it profitable to ship gold to Singapore. Either one or two things should be done. All remittances required for movements originating with the Commissioners, whether for the purchase of securities to bring up the investment portion to its statutory maximum or the gold portion to its legal maximum limit, should be made at current rates through the Banks, or they should be made at the gold import point through the Banks when the opportunity occurs, or effected by transport of gold to London. I recommend the first alternative. The amount to be remitted is known and limited, and as the issue of fresh money caused by remittances for investments has not created in the past much appreciable disturbance of the local money market, still less effect would it have in the case of remittances to feed the gold portion of the fund in London, limited, as it is, to one-third of the investment portion.

The demands of the public are on a very different footing from these domestic operations of the Currency Commissioners. The demand will only arise when exchange reaches either the import or export point. When it does come, it should be fully recognised that, with the exception of the minimum limit of the silver to be held in the Colony, no heed need be paid to the limits fixed by Statute to the different portions of the Guarantee Fund. So long as the demand continues, so long should it be satisfied to the utmost extent of the Colony's credit.

In the controversy, which took place between the Government on the one hand, and the Chamber of Commerce and the unofficial members of the Legislative Council on the other, regarding the proposal to make it lawful for the Currency Commissioners to buy transfers on London at any point between the parity of exchange and the gold import point, the distinction now pointed out between movements originating with the Currency Commissioners and movements originating with the public was not, I think, clearly recognised by either party. The Government wanted to obtain sufficient gold in London economically and expeditiously. The Chamber of Commerce and the unofficial members

of Council dreaded the effect on trade of the Banks
selling to Government as much gold as they could
lay their hands on, at current rates of exchange,
even with the proviso that the rates should be
confined between the par of exchange and import
point. The reasons given were that it would
interfere with the parity of exchange, if transfers
were effected below the gold import point, as what
fixed exchange was the rate at which notes were
issued for gold tendered locally, and that, if the cost
of transport were, by means of the rates allowed,
made lower than the actual cost, gold would not
flow into the Colony, and the dollar would have an
unstable value ranging between its declared value in
gold and the import point, and would fluctuate
within these limits with the fluctuations of the bank
rates of exchange; that such action would interfere
with the legitimate operations of the exchange banks
and would encourage Banks to work on dangerously
low balances. The Lords Commissioners of the
Treasury held the view that the grant of such
a power to the Currency Commissioners would
mean the exercise of their personal discretion, and
would interfere with the automatic working of the
scheme. They, too, overlooked the fact that
remittances for investments, which form a larger
part of the Guarantee Fund than gold, are made at
the current rates of exchange, and did not clearly
see the distinction which lies between operations,
which the Currency Commissioners may have to
make on their own initiative, and operations arising

from a public demand for the adjustment of trade balances. On the other hand, the Straits Government in making this proposal were not careful enough to define the limits within which their proposal should have been allowed to operate.

In India there are no statutory provisions for regulating the handling of the Gold Standard Reserve, and it would appear that remittances made at current rates of exchange have been freely made use of, for the purpose of replenishing the gold both in the Gold Standard Reserve and in the Paper Currency Reserve.

The procedure is as follows :—

Council Bills are sold between the gold points, but generally when exchange is favourable. The proceeds of these sales, though not made at the gold import point, have frequently been used to supply gold to the Paper Currency Reserve, when the Government required the release of rupees in India. Similarly, gold held in London on account of the Paper Currency Reserve has been withdrawn by the Secretary of State to supplement the sale of Council Bills, during periods of unfavourable exchange, for the Secretary of State's general requirements in England against the cancellation of notes held in the Government Treasuries in India or the transfer of rupees from those Treasuries to the Paper Currency Reserve in India. These transactions were apparently effected at par of exchange, though the Council Bills, the proceeds of which formed part of the gold accumulated in the

Paper Currency Reserve, were sold below the gold import point. Likewise with regard to the Gold Standard Reserve, the profits on coinage have been remitted to London through the medium of the sale of Council Bills; or, when the Secretary of State had to issue a loan or renew large blocks of debentures, bills and transfers sold by the Secretary of State were met by the Government of India from the rupees of the Indian Branch of the Gold Standard Reserve, the sale proceeds being added temporarily to the London Branch by the Secretary of State, so as to avoid any disturbance of the London market in the interests of the particular issue of a loan or the renewal of debentures. When exchange recovered after the crisis of 1907-8, the sales of Council Bills were used to replenish the gold, which had been taken out of the London Reserve during the crisis, and were met from the accumulation of rupees which had taken place in India by payment for the gold taken out in London. These Council Bills, too, were not sold at the gold import point.

This is a matter of very great importance to the Government of the Straits Settlements, for, if the view taken of these operations in India by such an authoritative body as the Royal Commission on Indian Currency and Finance were made applicable to the Straits Settlements, great economies would be effected. This must be my excuse for quoting in full the part of their Report dealing with this subject.

"We consider that the Government should

K

follow the market rate whenever it is profitable to do so. In other words, the propriety of the transactions of the Government in the exchange markets must be judged with reference to the urgency of their requirements and the rate obtainable.

"In what we have said so far we had in mind primarily the remittance of Treasury balances, but the same considerations apply also to Council drafts for the purpose of the Paper Currency or Gold Standard Reserves. It has been said that the system of selling Council drafts to be met from the Paper Currency Reserve in India originated in the desire to assist trade, when Government were unable to meet demands for remittance from their treasury, but it will be clear from what we have said that we do not regard this as a sufficient reason. The justification of such sales must be that, whether for the purchase of silver or for some other purpose, it is considered desirable to hold part of the Paper Currency Reserve in London. Similarly, in the case of the Gold Standard Reserve, the sale of Council drafts is proper in circumstances in which funds belonging to that reserve have to be transferred to London. In either case the real grounds for remittance must be the home requirements of the Government.

" We hold, therefore, that even in the case of the Paper Currency and Gold Standard Reserves, the Secretary of State must have discretion to draw within the limits of what are termed the gold points

at the rates obtainable when the remittance becomes
necessary. An instructive example of the need of
such discretion is supplied by the experience of
1909, when, after the crisis of the preceding two
years, a large amount belonging to the Gold
Standard Reserve had accumulated in India and
was remitted home at considerably below the par
of exchange. It has been urged that it would be
better, when funds belonging to the Gold Standard
Reserve are concerned, to defer remittance till a
rate above par can be obtained. But the first
necessity at such a time may be to get the funds to
London, as soon as possible, in order that they may
be available for use in case of any further disturbance of exchange, and we should be unwilling to
limit the discretion of the Secretary of State in such
circumstances.

" The opinion is often expressed that, while
ordinarily the question of rates may be treated on
the lines which we favour, further considerations
arise when the sales involve new coinage ; and it is
suggested that Council bills should not then be sold
below 1/4⅛. The suggestion, however, seems to
draw too sharp a distinction between the various
funds of the Government and the purposes to which
they are applied. It is always possible, for instance,
that the silver required for coinage may be purchased
from Treasury funds at home, a transfer being made
from the Paper Currency Reserve to the Treasury
in India when this silver is shipped and becomes
part of the Paper Currency Reserve, and Council

drafts in that case would have to be paid for sooner or later out of the Treasury to make good the home expenditure. Moreover, the suggestion has in view only the gold point as between India and England, whereas rupees may have to be given in exchange for gold imported at various rates from Egypt and Australia and elsewhere. Since further coinage becomes necessary only in times of active trade, exchange naturally tends to be high when fresh coinage is required. It is desirable that sales for the purpose of new coinage should be kept as closely as possible to specie point (whatever that point may be at the moment) ; but we think it undesirable to limit the Secretary of State's discretion by rigid rules.

"We sum up our views as follows: We cannot agree that the India Office should make a point of not selling drafts in any circumstances below gold point or below any arbitrarily-fixed rate. The general policy pursued at present is, in our view, the right one, viz., to regulate the time and amount of the sale of Council drafts throughout the year according to requirements, so as to take full advantage of the demand for such drafts in order to lay down funds in London. Though the convenience of trade and the regulation of exchange are important considerations for the India Office in the management of the system, we think that in some of the explanations of it given to the public too much stress has been laid upon this aspect and too little attention has been directed to the primary and by far the most important functions of Council drafts, viz., the transfer to London from India of public funds to meet the requirements of the Secretary of State in London. This is true not only of those Council drafts which are met from Treasury balances in India, and serve simply to transfer part of the cash balance from India to London, but also of those which are met from the Reserves in India, since the object of the sale of these drafts is to lay down in London such portions of the two Reserves as the Secretary of State and the Government of India desire to locate in London, either permanently, as in the case of the Gold Standard Reserve or the gold portion of the Paper Currency Reserve earmarked at the Bank of England, or temporarily as in the case of moneys belonging to the Paper Currency Reserve which are transferred to London for the purchase of silver for coinage. This is one of the points in which it is particularly important not to overlook the fact that the various funds concerned are, as we have said, really one single whole. If a broad view of the situation is taken, it can be said, without departing from accuracy, that Council drafts are sold for no other reason or to no larger amount than is necessary to meet the requirements, present or prospective, of the Secretary of State in London."

The Sale of Council Bills by the Secretary of State is the same operation as the purchase of remittances by the Government of the Straits Settlements for the transfer of their own funds, and the purchase of remittances by the Currency Commissioners for the transfer to London of portions of their reserve for investment. The recommendations of the Commission, if applied to the Straits, would amount to this. The Government of the Straits Settlements (which includes the Currency Commissioners) would be allowed to purchase drafts within the gold points within certain limits, viz., the home requirements of the Government. When exchange reaches the gold import point, the Government would be prepared to purchase drafts without limit from the public, and when exchange reaches the gold export point they would be prepared to the utmost limit of their gold and investment reserves in London, and, if necessary, to the utmost limit of their credit to sell drafts on London to the public, besides giving out the gold in Singapore on the condition that it is exported. It will be seen that the first of these measures is a great extension of the proposal of the Straits Government, viz., the proposal to buy remittances, for the home requirements of the Currency Commissioners, only between the par of exchange and the import point.

The system adopted in Java affords instructive lessons. They seem to have advanced a stage further than India or the Straits, the control of the currency with the duty of maintaining exchange being relegated to a central or State Bank, known to us as the Java Bank. In 1891 the Bank was allowed to hold part of its assets in Holland and abroad. All remittances required by Government between Holland and Netherlands-Indies were entrusted to the Java Bank, and are made by the Bank at the par of exchange without profit or loss to the Government. It has charge of the note issue, and keeps the reserves against it, as detailed in the preceding chapter. The functions of the Bank is that of a Banker's bank. It does not, therefore, compete in the market with the Exchange Banks for foreign bills of exchange, but only enters the market when it requires transfers for its private needs in connection with the published policy of the Bank, or for the disposal of its balances; otherwise it buys and sells drafts and telegraphic transfers on foreign countries as near the gold points as possible, places specie at the disposal of the public for export abroad when the specie export point is reached, and buys imported gold when the rate of exchange reaches import point. An important feature of the management of this bank is the amount of foreign credits acquired by it in England, France, and Germany, both by financing other banks and discounting direct produce bills in Java. Such foreign credits are perhaps handier than gold located at a distance for the liquidation of adverse trade balances, and can also be used for the purchase of gold when required. The policy of the bank is to supply remittances limited only by the extent of its credit to the public at the gold import and export point, and to deal at market rates for the supply of its own requirements. Here, too, the procedure is similar to what obtains in India and what has now been definitely authorized by the Royal Commission.

The offer of the Government to issue notes in exchange for gold tendered in Singapore did not have the effect of assuring fixity of exchange, but placed an upper limit to the appreciation of the gold value of the dollar; for the value cannot exceed the par of exchange plus the cost of transport of gold, without gold being imported into Singapore. This is what is known as the import gold point, which varies with the cost of freight, insurance, and interest, but as these are fairly uniform, except in times of war, the limit fixed, viz., $2/4\frac{5}{16}$—afterwards reduced to $2/4\frac{3}{16}$—was definitely assured for normal periods, as the Government could not find much difficulty in keeping sufficient stocks of notes and dollars to meet all demands.* The only complication which they had to face was the importation of gold from countries other than England, such as Australia and Egypt, from which countries, and occasionally from England, the Banks have been able to procure gold at a laying-down price of $2/4\frac{1}{8}$, $\frac{1}{16}$th less than the point at which Government are prepared to buy sterling drafts. Shipments are also made from India, China, and Japan at a price materially below this, but no measures are possible

---

* The reason why the import and export points were not fixed at points equidistant from the par of exchange is that the import point ($2/4\frac{3}{16}$) represents the cost of importing gold from Australia where the gold usually comes from, and the export point ($2/3\frac{11}{16}$) represents the cost of exporting gold to London, where it is usually required.

to divert such shipments to London without loss to Government, and as they have hitherto not been made in considerable amounts, the question has not become one of very great importance.

The principle, underlying the scheme for the diversion to London of shipments of gold from Australia and Egypt intended for Singapore, and which would have come to Singapore except for such diversion, is that the transport of such gold to London should be effected at the import point of gold to Singapore from the countries exporting. If, therefore, the cost of sending gold to London from Australia or Egypt is greater than the cost of sending it to Singapore, the Government should and does bear the extra cost. If less, it is correct in theory that the Government should get the difference. In practice, however, the Government is satisfied if the diversion is made without any loss to them, the only condition being that the shipment of gold shall be convertible into local currency at the par of exchange immediately on the expiry of the period which it would take the gold to reach Singapore by the approved and usual routes from the country of export. If the import point to Singapore is less than the import point to London, the Government makes good the difference. If the import point to Singapore is greater than the import point to London, the importer keeps the difference. As a matter of fact, the import point to Singapore and London from Australia is, in normal circumstances, practically the same, but the import point to London from Egypt is less than the import point to Singapore from that country. Practically the scheme takes no regard of the cost of transport, but only of the time which would be taken to deliver the gold at Singapore. If the scheme, as it is worked, were applied to gold lying in London which a Bank wished to convert into Straits currency at Singapore, and the Straits Government wished to keep in London, the Bank would be able to get Straits currency at Singapore in thirty days, viz., the time taken by a P. and O. steamer to arrive at Singapore from London, after delivery of the gold in London to the Crown Agents for the Colonies, that is to say, with loss of one month's interest only, without incurring any expense for the cost of transport. In practice, however, as regards gold lying in London, a transfer can only be made at $2/4\frac{3}{16}$, the gold import point fixed by the Government for the time being, or by the actual transfer of gold from London to Singapore.

It is apparent, therefore, that the scheme, as it is worked, does not secure the maintenance of the principle that remittances should be made at the gold import point, though it must be admitted that it is automatic in its operation. If the practice were continued to let the importer keep what difference there is in his favour in the cost of transport, it would be logical to deal with the gold lying in London intended for Singapore on the same lines as the gold in transit from Australia and Egypt, viz., to issue local currency to the importer on the advertised date of the arrival of the mail steamer next leaving London after the delivery of the gold, and not take into account the cost of transport. The distinction, however, should be kept in mind, in considering this complicated question, between Australian gold on the one hand and London and Egyptian gol on the other. Australia is a gold-producing country, whereas the gold in Egypt and London is imported gold, and has already borne the cost of its import in addition to the cost of production ; and, as a rule, it should be easier to get gold from Australia laid down in Singapore than either from Egypt or London. It would not be feasible, however, to accumulate gold in London under this scheme, if the importer gained nothing by acceding to the wishes of the Government to divert gold in transit to London ; and here, again, it is evident that the rigid rule of adhering to the gold points, that some theorists consider so absolutely necessary for the automatic working of our currency scheme, has been departed from in this substitution of purchase of gold in transit for purchase of remittances at gold import point, or the actual importation of gold. So that it comes to this, that, under this scheme as well, the Government, when they required gold in London for their own purposes, have made the best arrangements possible, and have followed the ruling of the Royal Commission, which I have already quoted, as regards the laying down of gold in London for the Government's home requirements.

We have seen that the issue of local currency in Singapore for gold locally tendered at the par of exchange automatically fixes the upper limit to which exchange can reach. We will now proceed to examine the measures taken, or which were rather forced upon Government, to fix the lower limit, viz., to make the gold export point the limit below which the dollar should not be allowed to fall. The Straits Settlements' Currency Committee of 1903 recommended (see paragraph 61) that the Government should be prepared to give sovereigns in exchange for dollars at the fixed rate, so long as gold is available, or to give bills on the Crown Agents in London based on that rate. In the same year the Advisory Sub-Committee appointed by the Singapore Chamber of Commerce pointed out that the Government would require to give gold or demand bills, or telegraphic transfers on London, in exchange for the new dollars, to prevent the rate falling below the fixed rate, and that otherwise there would be no sufficient guarantee against a serious decline in exchange. At the end of the year the Secretary of State, whilst authorizing the issue of notes in Singapore against gold tendered to the Crown Agents in London at a rate of exchange to be notified by order of the Governor in Council with the view of guarding against the danger of an excessive rise in the exchange value of the dollar, definitely laid down that there would be no need to make any provision for the issue of gold by the Currency Commissioners in exchange for notes, since, although the ultimate effective continuance of the gold standard would depend on the ability of the Currency Commissioners to give gold or gold drafts on the Crown Agents, there would be no legal obligation on them to do so; and that, therefore, they need not be empowered to give gold, since they would only issue it when desired. The question was not raised again till 1905, and it was not considered necessary to take any action, as it was then thought that the only sound course was the issue of notes in Singapore against gold tendered there, and that, by the adoption of this course, exchange would fluctuate in the normal manner between . England and the Straits Settlements within the limits imposed by shipping gold in each direction. That is to say, that the operation of issuing notes against gold tendered locally at the fixed rate was considered to be sufficient to fix automatically the upper and lower limits for the fluctuation of the exchange value of the dollar. It was announced that the Government would buy, but not sell gold, and this position continued till 1906, when representations were made by the Governor that the issue of notes against gold would only fix the upper limit, and that to fix the downward limit it would be necessary to sell gold. It was requested that the Government should be empowered to sell transfers within certain limits, viz., to the extent of £100,000, but not exceeding £50,000 in any week, and to give out gold in excess of £100,000 in the possession of the Currency

Commissioners. The Lords Commissioners of the Treasury, while fully recognising that it was the duty of the Government to take reasonable steps to prevent the dollar from falling away from the intended rate, and while approving the proposal to retire Government notes for this purpose by the issue of gold, in case of necessity, to the full extent of the reserve, were strongly of opinion that, in the event of the failure of this measure to restore exchange, the sale of telegraphic transfers on London should not be made the subject of a general authority, but that the Government of the Colony should rely on their control over the supply of the dollar to avert the danger. It was accordingly agreed that the Government should give out gold, if desired, to the full extent of its reserve, and, in the event of the gold being exhausted, and exchange still remaining below specie point, the question of selling telegraphic transfers should be specially referred to the Secretary of State. Finally, in September, 1906, the Currency Commissioners were empowered by law to issue gold in exchange for notes at the fixed rate, and to accept tenders for the purchase of telegraphic transfers payable in London by the Crown Agents, which would afford a sufficient margin below the rate fixed to cover all charges, including interest, which may be incurred in remitting to London the equivalent in gold at the fixed rate of the notes received for such tender. By legislative sanction being thus given to the issue of gold locally, and the sale of telegraphic transfers by Government on the Crown Agents in London, the limitation of the downward trend of the dollar was definitely assured. We have seen how this measure triumphantly stood the test to which our currency scheme was subjected in the crisis of 1907-1908.

This system, in its material points, is what is known in India as the Lindsay scheme, and its adoption was forced on the Straits Government to save their new currency arrangements from collapse. The reluctance of the Government in the early stages was reasonable, and can easily be understood. Under the original scheme on which our currency was based, viz., the substitution of a special Straits dollar of exactly the same weight and fineness as the British dollars in currency, and owing to the use of the old dollars in the Currency Commissioners' reserve for conversion into the new, no profits from seignorage could be expected for the formation of a gold reserve fund. Further, it was not anticipated that notes would so largely displace dollars as to enable the Government to release such considerable quantities of dollars, as they afterwards did, for sale as bullion and conversion into gold. In the early stages there were no resources open to Government except the realisation of the Currency Commissioners' investments, whose primary purpose was to secure the convertibility of the notes; and it was apparent that, in the absence of a gold reserve, sterling bills on the Crown Agents would have to be met by advances from general revenue.

The hesitation of the Government to take upon themselves an obligation to sell transfers on the Crown Agents is, therefore, easily explainable. When the time came and the Government were obliged to take this step, it was fortunate for them that they happened to be in possession of considerable loan moneys for which they had no immediate use ; but a secure position was only attained after the conversion into gold of the profits of the seignorage from the coinage of the smaller dollar, and from the proceeds of sale of the large stocks of old dollars displaced from circulation by notes. The borrowings from the surplus loan funds were repaid from this source, and a substantial balance remained to form an adequate coin reserve of gold. The effective establishment of the system of remittances for the support of exchange was therefore due to the rise in the price of silver.

It will not be out of place to discuss here the question of the alternative measure, suggested by the Lords Commissioners of the Treasury, that the Government should rely on their control of the supply of the dollar to prevent the dollar from falling away from the intended rate.

This proposal was made by Ricardo, as has been seen in the previous chapter, in regard to maintaining the value of paper currency without keeping a reserve. The position of the dollar, except for the value of its silver content, is exactly the same as that of the note. It is a token with a definite gold value attached to it. The theory is, that as exchange rises or falls, or as dollar prices fall and rise, the relative value with gold of the local currency can be maintained by increasing or reducing the amount of unlimited legal tender silver in circulation. There are two ways of doing this which can be made use of either independently or supplementary one to the other. When exchange is high by coining and issuing new dollars, and by increasing the Government accounts with the Banks from the Treasuries and Sub-Treasuries. The latter method will hardly make any appreciable difference to the situation, as nearly all Government moneys, both in the Straits and the Federated Malay States, are lodged with the Banks, and the amounts kept in the Treasuries are small in comparison. Both these matters depend to some extent on the exercise of the personal judgment of the Currency Commissioners, and are not so automatic in their operation as the use of remittances.

Except for the purpose of keeping the local silver reserve at its statutory limit, the Government are not likely to be called upon to undertake any fresh coinage of dollars, as any required expansion of currency will be in the form of notes, and not of silver, and if silver is issued, it will be returned to Government for exchange into notes, with the result that the gold reserve will diminish in proportion.

When a contraction of currency is required when exchange is low, if remittances are not freely made use of, the only method open to Government is to withdraw their Bank balances and lock up their

L

revenue, as it comes in, in the different Government Treasuries, or to raise loans to take off the surplus dollars from the market. These are not methods which can be recommended. They involve the exercise of a personal discretion on the part of the Currency Commissioners.

It may be mentioned that the method of increasing or reducing Government balances in the Banks has been made use of, not as an alternative to buying and selling remittances, but as supplementary to it. It is not of itself a sufficiently powerful weapon to have much effect on the fluctuations of exchange, but its use during the crisis of 1907-8 effectually lessened the applications for the purchase of sterling bills from the Currency Commissioners.

CHAPTER VII

THE VALUE OF STANDARD IN RELATION TO FOREIGN TRADE

"TIME," says Mr. Keynes in his book on Indian Currency and Finance, "has muffled the outcries of the silver interests, and time has also dealt satisfactorily with one of the principle grounds of criticism, viz., that a depreciating currency is advantageous to a country's foreign trade." He states that the criticisms of 1893 are no longer heard.

The experience of the Straits Settlements has been very different. This criticism is now being urged with greater persistency than ever, and there is a perceptible movement at present to secure a reduction of the value of the dollar to two shillings. This feeling in favour of a reduction has been voiced in the Press and by the Planters' representative at the last dinner of the Straits Settlements Association, and it is receiving favourable consideration in influential quarters in the Colony.

The reduction of the gold value of the unit from its present value, after an existence of nine years, will bring such serious consequences in its train that the question should be considered not in relation to the effects it would have on any particular industry or trade, but in the interests of the community as a whole. The relations between debtor and creditor, which are now founded on a stable basis, will be seriously disturbed, and much harm will be done to the large import business of the Colony and the Malay States. Another change in our currency will also tend to disturb profoundly public confidence in the Government. Prices are adjusting themselves to the standard of value established in 1906, and that they have not done so more quickly is due to the evil effects of the rubber boom, when the sudden accession of wealth resulted in the enhancement of prices of most commodities, of wages, and of salaries. Money being abundant and easily obtainable, people did not mind what they paid for labour and material so long as the margin of profit left them was more than was sufficient for their utmost needs. Now that the pinch has come and the strictest economy is necessary to maintain this industry as a paying concern, the complaint is that the Malay Peninsula, owing to the higher standard of value adopted for their unit, is in an unfavourable position as compared with Ceylon and Java, where the gold value of the unit is much lower.

Economists have pointed out that all trade is in its essence barter, that the use of money serves only as a common ground for the comparison of the values of different commodities, and is a contrivance to diminish friction, that, in a barter system, trade gravitates to the point at which the sum of the imports exactly exchanges for the sum of the exports, and that, in a money system, it gravitates to the point at which the sum of the imports and the sum of the exports exchange for the same quantity of money. It has been explained that the trade between two countries is governed by the relative cost of producing commodities in one country as compared with the relative cost of producing or procuring the same commodities in the other, that it is not permanently affected by the value of the standard coin of the countries in question, and that any advantage to exporters caused by a fall in the value of the standard can only be temporary, and is obtained at the expense of the rest of the community.

Instances are given both in Mr. Keynes' book on Indian Currency and Finance (see pages 3 and 4), and in Sir David Barbour's work on the Standard of Value (see pages 172-4 and 196-7), drawn from Indian experience in support of these contentions. The Herschell Committee, after an investigation of statistics between 1871 and 1879, recorded their conclusion that the progress of the export trade had been less with a rapidly-falling than with a steady exchange.

Let us see what the experience of the Straits Settlements has been in the matter.

The Sub-Committee of the Singapore Chamber of

Commerce, appointed in 1897, make the following remarks on this question in their report :—

" It is believed to be a prevailing idea amongst some Chinese merchants in the Straits that the effect of the fall in the gold value of the dollar has been to enhance local prices of produce sold by them, and that they, therefore, as sellers, have benefited by the decline ; but if the course of prices from 1890 to 1896 (appendix D.)* is studied, it will be seen that, on the whole, producers have not only not benefited, but are actually in a worse position, with a dollar below 2s., than they were when the value of the coin was above 3s.

" Those who have followed the course of the Singapore produce market, during the period referred to, cannot but admit that prices are really only temporarily affected by any fluctuations in exchange, viz., that a sudden drop or a rapid rise merely causes a temporary rise or fall in the value of any article of produce, and that eventually prices do readjust themselves according to the usual laws of supply and demand. On the other hand, it has to be admitted that the effect of the decline in exchange—more rapid as a rule than the corresponding fall in the gold value of produce in Europe and elsewhere—has undoubtedly been to enormously stimulate production, and this has naturally been a source of profit to the Colony, and to the Peninsula, although the individual producer may have suffered. The Sub-Committee have, therefore, to take this

* Not printed.

into consideration in their recommendations, and, in suggesting fixity, the aim should be to give the dollar such gold value as ruled when the trade of the Colony was in its most flourishing condition as regards volume of exports.

Appendix F* gives some details regarding the movements of various articles of produce during the years under review, and the total exports of those articles in each year, from 1890 to 1896. From those figures it will be seen that the year 1896 generally shows the largest exports, and the average value of the dollar for that year was as nearly as possible 2/2⅛.

"It is alleged that tin miners were more prosperous in 1890 than in 1896, and that any temporary advance in dollar price during that period was counteracted by a more than corresponding increase in the cost of labour and food, and was lost by over-production. In 1896 many miners were forced to suspend operations, and, from investigations, your Committee were led to believe that depreciation of the dollar has not benefited produce except temporarily."

Five years later, in a letter addressed to the Colonial Secretary by the Singapore Chamber of Commerce, the following observations are made on the same subject: "I am directed to particularly draw the attention of Government to the figures as to exports shown by schedules 4 to 6. From these figures it will be seen that for the year 1897 the

* Not printed.

trade figures (inter. settlements excluded) were as follows :—

1897. $160,851,000.
1898. $184,970,000.
1899. $215,888,000.
1900. $232,622,000.
1901. $245,069,000.

" It has, by some people, been contended that this increased dollar volume of the trade is due to the declining value of our local currency.

" The increases, however, shown by the figures just above quoted, occurred under what was practically a period of fixity of exchange, as is shown by the following, which were the average rates on London for these years :—

1897.	1898	1899.	1990.	1901.
$1.11\frac{15}{16}$	$1.11\frac{5}{16}$	$1.11\frac{15}{16}$	$2.0\frac{1}{2}$	$1.11\frac{11}{16}$

" Appendix F*, accompanying this letter, is a memorandum on the course of the produce (export) markets of Singapore during the years 1897-1901 inclusive; and from this it would seem reasonable to conclude that the increased dollar value in our export trade of these five years should not be placed to the credit of a declining dollar.

" Even if it be admitted that a dollar of low value had stimulated and increased the export trade of this

* Not printed.

Colony, it must also be accepted that in the course of decline a point must be reached, after which further decline must, in a general or over-all way, result in injury. If this be not admitted, then he who advocates that increased general prosperity must follow any decline of the dollar, would hold that a dollar fallen to 6d. (if that be possible) would be of benefit to the trade of the Colony and of the Peninsula. Under no circumstances could such a view or contention be upheld; it requires no argument or figures to demonstrate that a turning point must be reached at which benefit becomes transformed into injury.

"It has been argued by some that the decline of exchange has benefited the coolie class who, coming from China, mainly constitute the labouring classes of the Settlements and the Federated Malay States. It requires but little local knowledge to know that the dollar, in its now shrunken value, can only buy for the coolie much less than it was able to do when it was of a higher gold value. The Chinese of the Colony have certainly suffered by the fall in exchange, in that for the now depreciated dollar they can buy less food, less clothing, less land, less labour or service, less everything than its former value was able to procure, or, in other words, for these they now have to pay more dollars."

On the other hand, it is only fair to record that of the witnesses who gave evidence before the Straits Settlements Currency Committee, the conviction was firmly held by some of the most experienced that a low standard of value directly stimulated exports, and made trades possible which were impossible under a higher standard. One of the most eminent bankers in the Far East, in speaking of the growth of certain branches of industry in China, stated : " Here is an article which is exported largely from China now—hides, and tallow, and things of that kind that were impossible to be exported long ago when we had a 4/- exchange. There are a hundred and one things exported from China now that were impossible twenty-five or thirty years ago." Many factors seem to me to be ignored here, more economical methods of preparing these articles for the market, cheaper transport, the nature of the demand for the manufactured articles from this material, improved methods of manufacture, and new uses.

Australia is a country with a gold standard, and yet we have seen many new industries started and developed there in quite as remarkable a manner. The development of the meat, butter, and fruit trades cannot be attributed to a depreciating currency. The fact is that the commercial possibilities of these trades were either not seen or not known in the early days referred to. To the demand that has arisen in foreign countries for these articles must be attributed the growth and development of the trade in them, and the increase of the demand for her exports enabled China to obtain more cheaply her imports from other countries as measured by the value of the commodities she was able to set against them.

The argument that high prices stimulate home industries is an old and familiar one, and was used by the now discredited advocates of an inconvertible paper currency. It was maintained that an increase of paper currency would produce a rise of prices, that the rise of prices would encourage the growth of industries, and give employment to capital and labour. As has been pointed out by Mill, times of speculation were mistaken for times of prosperity, the speculators did not think they were growing rich because the high prices would last, but because they would not last, and because whoever contrived to realise why they did last, would find himself, after the recoil, in possession of a greater number of pounds sterling, without their having become of less value. If, at the close of the speculation, an issue of paper had been made, sufficient to keep prices up to the point which they attained when at the highest, no one would have been more disappointed than the speculators. There is no way, he says, in which a general and permanent rise of prices, or, in other words, depreciation of money, can benefit anybody, except at the expense of somebody else. The substitution of paper for metallic currency is a national gain; any further increase of paper beyond this is but a form of robbery.

Similarly the reduction of the exchange value of the dollar will be to benefit a particular section of the community at the expense of the rest no less deserving; and when prices have adjusted themselves to the new value, the cry will be heard again, when times are unfavourable, that the standard is too high as compared with the Indian rupee and the Java guilder.

Another factor, which must not be overlooked, is that the adoption of a 2/- dollar might result in the use of gold as a currency medium for internal purposes, a policy which it would be against the interest of the Colony to encourage.

INDEX

R. W. SIMPSON AND CO., LTD. PRINTERS, RICHMOND, LONDON.

Lightning Source UK Ltd.
Milton Keynes UK
UKHW032150090223
416755UK00009B/669